# THE CALL TO RADICAL FAITHFULNESS

Presented

by the

H. H. Mosher Fund

of

New York

Yearly Meeting

# THE CALL TO RADICAL FAITHFULNESS

Covenant in Quaker Experience

Douglas Gwyn

Plain Press

ISBN: 1548140589
ISBN 13: 9781548140588

# TABLE OF CONTENTS

Introduction · · · · · · · · · · · · · · · · · · · · · · · · · · · · · · · · · · · · · · · · · ·vii

## Part I
### Answering the Call to Radical Faithfulness

1   Answering the Call to Radical Faithfulness: Some Early
Quaker Examples· · · · · · · · · · · · · · · · · · · · · · · · · · · · · · · · · · · 3

2   The Passion of James Parnell · · · · · · · · · · · · · · · · · · · · · · · · · ·11

3   John Burnyeat and Cumberland Friends: Crossing the
Red Sea in 1653· · · · · · · · · · · · · · · · · · · · · · · · · · · · · · · · · · · 15

4   Sarah Jones, Sarah Blackborow, and Francis Howgill:
Learning to Stay at Home with Jacob · · · · · · · · · · · · · · · · · ·21

5   George Fox to His Parents: "You Have No Time but This
Present Time" · · · · · · · · · · · · · · · · · · · · · · · · · · · · · · · · · · · · 30

6   George Fought the Battle of Jericho: Kendal, 1652 · · · · · · · · · · · 34

7   To the Peacemakers: "Let the Waves Break over Your Heads" · · · ·41

8   James Nayler and the Lamb's War: "Led by the Lamb in a
Way They Know Not"· · · · · · · · · · · · · · · · · · · · · · · · · · · · · · ·45

9   John Camm's Brilliant Failure · · · · · · · · · · · · · · · · · · · · · · · · ·53

10   George Fox's Dying Words: "I'm Glad I Was Here"· · · · · · · · · · ·57

## Part II
### Quaker Faith and Practice: A Covenantal Life

11   Covenant in Quaker Spiritual Formation · · · · · · · · · · · · · · · · ·63

12   Covenant in Quaker Worship, Ministry, and Decision-Making· · · ·72

13     Covenant and Testimony· · · · · · · · · · · · · · · · · · · · · · · · · · · · · ·79
14     Can't See the Covenant for the Contracts · · · · · · · · · · · · · · · · · 86
Coda Hospitality: The Practice of Covenantal Faithfulness · · · · · · · · · · · ·93

Notes· · · · · · · · · · · · · · · · · · · · · · · · · · · · · · · · · · · · · · · · · · · 99

# INTRODUCTION

*All existence is calling.*

—MARTIN BUBER

THIS LITTLE BOOK is comprised of a series of Bible Half-Hours I gave in August 2016 at New England Yearly Meeting, held at Castleton College in Vermont, interspersed with a series of related messages I offered that summer at Durham (Maine) Friends Meeting, where I was serving as a pastoral minister. Part II is material I shared while co-leading a short course with Ben Pink Dandelion on Quakers and covenant spirituality in August 2015 at the Woodbrooke Quaker Study Centre in Birmingham England.

"We Are God's Hands: The Call to Radical Faithfulness" was the theme of the New England Yearly Meeting sessions in 2016. When invited to bring the Bible Half-Hours for the sessions, I was led to use stories and writings from early Friends to show how the Bible framed their understanding of God's call; and conversely, how following that call into radical faithfulness gave them fresh readings of Scripture. As I was developing the talks for that series, I was inspired to tell some other stories from early Quaker history in messages I prepared for worship at Durham Meeting. I've included here ones relating to the themes of the Bible Half-Hours. The Half-Hours are reproduced here in Chapters 1, 3, 4, 6, and 8. The messages offered at Durham Meeting are reproduced here in Chapters 2, 5, 7, 9, and 10. They are noticeably shorter, as appropriate to a semi-programmed meeting for worship.

The concepts of divine calling and human-divine faithfulness are derived from the covenant theology of the Hebrew and Christian Scriptures. Since the covenant logic of Quaker faith and practice is largely forgotten among Friends today, it seemed useful to include the Woodbrooke material here as a Part 2, Chapters 11-13. Finally, Chapter 14 is a reprint, with minor editing and updating, of an article on covenant published in the May 1997 issue of *Friends Journal*. It also appeared in a collection of smaller pieces, *Words in Time*.[1] The article provides a fitting restatement of this book's themes of covenant, calling, and faithfulness. A brief coda concludes the book with reflections on hospitality as covenant faithfulness.

Excepting the final chapter, all these chapters originated as oral communication, making them shorter and less fleshed-out than they might otherwise have been. But I've chosen to retain the form in which they were presented (with minor editing), hoping that their brief, allusive quality will suffice for readers as it did for many listeners. Those interested in the fuller story of early Friends and their covenant theology can find it much more fully developed in my trilogy of books on the early Quaker movement: *Apocalypse of the Word: The Life and Message of George Fox* (1986); *The Covenant Crucified: Quakers and the Rise of Capitalism* (1995); and *Seekers Found: Atonement in Early Quaker Experience* (2000). Much of the material in these chapters is drawn from those books.

In this new century, we find ourselves awash in the global, instantaneous Now of Internet communications and information. Friends are no exception. While this situation presents endless opportunities for doing good, we would be wise to remember that information does not provide the frameworks of understanding that make information useful in discerning our way. And we all know how electronic communication can simply proliferate, unless we exert serious discernment. Scripture and Quaker tradition offer a rich treasury of interpretive frameworks, which Friends ignore at our peril. G. K. Chesterton called tradition "democracy extended through time." In counterpoint, a rabbi sojourning at Pendle Hill once shared with me a motto of the Reconstructionist stream of Judaism: "Tradition has a vote, but not a veto."

Listening to earlier generations of Friends can enrich our faith and our sense of faithful possibility in the present. Like stories from the Bible, many of these Quaker stories come from times very different from our own. They can only serve as parables, archetypes, figures, examples that model for us lives of radical faithfulness. Therefore, our own faithful experiments can *confirm* their truth without necessarily *conforming* to the details.

I want to thank Durham Friends Meeting for their warm friendship and their encouragement of my ministry among them over the past two years. I also thank the Program Committee for the 2016 sessions of New England Yearly Meeting for the invitation to bring the Bible Half-Hours. It stimulated a fruitful process of research, reflection, and writing. I want thank Ben Pink Dandelion for his prophetic 2014 Swarthmore Lecture and his suggestion that we teach the Woodbrooke course together as a follow-up to it. Ben's friendship and collaboration have been a blessing to me—and to many others—over the years. Emily Savin edited and proof-read the manuscript with her usual grace and aplomb. Finally, I wish to thank Philadelphia Friend Esther Murer for gently encouraging me for some years to distil my trilogy on early Friends into something shorter and less demanding. This may be it.

Douglas Gwyn
Pendle Hill
June 2017

# PART I

## ANSWERING THE CALL TO RADICAL FAITHFULNESS

# 1

## ANSWERING THE CALL TO RADICAL FAITHFULNESS: SOME EARLY QUAKER EXAMPLES

WHEN I WAS invited to give the Bible Half-Hours at New England Yearly Meeting's 2016 sessions, the Planning Committee asked me to begin with some stories of early Friends that illustrate answering the call to radical faithfulness. As it has turned out, the whole series of these half-hours will be early Quaker stories. These stories illustrate not only answering the call to radical faithfulness, but ways in which early Friends read the Bible. Not only did the Bible frame the way they understood their call: in turn, their experience of answering the call also gave them fresh insights into Scripture. As we follow the journeys of these early Friends, living a mere three and a half centuries ago, we may find a helpful bridge to a fresh reading of the ancient texts of the Bible for ourselves. And still further, we may open ourselves to being read by the Bible.

Early Friends had a clarity that inspires many of us. Often, clarity is born out of *crisis*, when you don't have the luxury to say, well, maybe this, maybe that. Friends emerged at the end of the English Civil War of the 1640s, a time of intense national crisis. And that crisis extended through the 1650s, as England drifted on, unsettled in both politics and religion. Early Friends were young men and women who lived that crisis intensely. During the war, before they became Quakers, some had served in Parliament's army. Others had been Seekers, church dropouts who participated in a variety of experimental worship groups. We might call most of them hyper-Puritans. They ached for authentic, transforming experience of God, to live lives of radical faithfulness, and to be part of an authentic church.

There were thousands of such Seekers in England by the end of the Civil War. But as the 1650s unfolded, most people were weary of the crisis and worried for the future of the nation and its church. Many just wanted to return to the comfortable verities of life as usual. So, when Quakers appeared on the scene, they made themselves very unpopular because they kept ramping up the crisis.

Our word "crisis" derives from the Greek *krisis,* which also means judgment, a time for decision. *Hypocrisy* is what happens when we prefer comfort over crisis. Hypocrisy means, literally, not enough crisis in your life, a superficial level of discernment, an evasion of the hard decisions. Hypocrisy is what happens when we repress the truth too long and in too many ways—a truth that keeps welling up from somewhere deep within.

So let's look at some early Quaker stories to see how that crisis played out in their lives, how they answered the call to radical faithfulness, and how it informed the way they read the Bible.

I'll begin with **George Fox.** He was not the only gifted leader of the Quaker movement, but he seems to be the one who lit the fire under the others, and continued to be most central and influential among them in the years to come.

George was still just 19 years old when he finally left home in 1643, when he could no longer abide the hypocrisy and comfortable religion of his village in the English midlands. The Civil War was underway, and young George was one of a growing phenomenon of Seekers. These were not "happy seekers." They were tormented souls, wandering the countryside and seeking answers.

Young George looked for answers in a variety of books, teachers, and experimental groups. But, as he records it, he could find "none that could speak to my condition." Finally, in his early 20s, he gave up looking for the next big thing out there, just around the next corner, and found his true teacher within: "There is one, even Christ Jesus, that can speak to thy condition."[2] This inward teacher began to redirect his attention and transform his life. And over time, George learned how to lead others to that same source within. By the latter 1640s, he was founding small, quiet worship groups around the midlands. They called themselves Children of the Light. They didn't attract much attention or trouble, though Fox had a few confrontations and one arrest in those early days.

But in October 1650, young George, now 26, made an exploratory trip further north, to the town of Derby. He came upon a religious discussion among some soldiers stationed there (Parliament's army was full of religious radicals). George was inspired to tell them about the light within and how it can lead a person to overcome sin in this life. This perfectionist teaching was blasphemy to orthodox Puritans. One of the officers took him by the arm and led him away to appear before a judge. To his surprise, he was sentenced to six months in prison for blasphemy. But George didn't take this as a defeat or a setback. He writes that he felt the spirit in him doubled. And from his cell, George laid siege to the town of Derby. He set out to make his crisis Derby's crisis. He debated local ministers in his cell; he wrote public letters to town leaders. Most of all, he announced that the day of the Lord, a time of divine visitation, had dawned upon the town of Derby.

Just as his six-month sentence was almost over, the Parliamentary army tried to recruit him. When George flatly refused, he found himself in jail for another six months. Like Brer Rabbit thrown in the briar patch, young George was just getting stronger and stronger. When he was finally released in October 1651, after a year in prison, the town of Derby was glad to be rid of him. But for his part, George writes that he felt like a lion coming out of its den and moving among the beasts of the forest.[3] A year before, trouble had found young George in a way that surprised him. Now he was out looking for it.

Over the next year, Fox, still only 28, gathered a group of traveling prophets—gifted women and men who would multiply and extend his spiritual teaching. They called themselves the Valiant Sixty. They clearly understood themselves in the light of the gospel story of Jesus sending out seventy disciples in pairs to preach and heal around the countryside (Luke 10).

Living the crisis, living the day of the Lord, they began living the biblical stories as their own story. With incredible energy and speed, they gathered thousands into this spreading crisis, drawing people together under the direct teaching and leadership of Christ's light. The movement grew exponentially in these early years and shook the social order around them. They announced the day of the Lord as a day of crisis and decision, not just in religious life but in all aspects of society (more about that in later chapters).

**James Nayler** was one of the earliest allies Fox found in this work. James was a Yorkshire farmer, married with three daughters. He had served as a quartermaster in the Parliamentary army during the war and was an admired preacher among the ranks. He left the army in 1650 and returned to his farm and family. By 1651, while Fox was still in prison in Derby, Nayler was in his mid-30s and part of a small group of radicals in his area. Fox's imprisonment had drawn their attention and they were in correspondence with him even before his release. After he was freed, Fox quickly made his way to meet with this group. There was a powerful convergence among them. The Yorkshire group added an element of social radicalism not found in the Children of the Light groups that Fox had gathered earlier. For his part, Fox offered a spiritual counsel that set these radicals on fire. Before Fox arrived, they were just sitting around wondering what to do. Soon they were setting the whole countryside on fire.

The following spring, in 1652, Nayler was still on the farm with his family, getting ready for another growing season. But while he was out plowing his fields, he felt a distinct call to join in this new ministry. He started making arrangements to leave home, but then he balked. When he fell ill, he was sure that God was chastising him for not heeding the call. So as he recovered, he resumed preparations to leave. But how could he leave a farm, a wife, and three daughters?

One day later that spring, he simply walked out the front gate and kept going, wearing old clothes, carrying no money, not even saying goodbye, and with no destination in mind. He later testified, "Ever since I have remained, not knowing today what I was to do tomorrow."[4]

Clearly, Nayler had stopped reading the gospels as inspiring stories from long ago. He took his place alongside those first disciples of Jesus who dropped their nets, who turned from their plows, and answered the call to radical faithfulness. The *history* of the Bible became fused with the *mystery* of his inward teacher and became one powerful story of crisis and transformation.

Another of Fox's most important early allies was **Margaret Fell**. Her moment of crisis came in June 1652. She was 38 years old and mother of a large family. She and her husband, Judge Thomas Fell, had for many years opened their large home, Swarthmoor Hall, to all kinds of traveling preachers. When Fox came along, he was just one more. She invited him to come to services at her local parish church in Ulverston. Fox asked permission to speak and started talking about the light of Christ in the human conscience. This was a new idea to Margaret. But George pressed the point further, beyond an idea, to a crisis, a moment of decision. As Margaret reports it,

> He said, "What have any of you to do with the Scriptures, but as you come to the Spirit that inspired the Scriptures? You will say, Christ saith this, and the apostles say this; but what canst thou say? Art thou a child of the Light and hast walked in the Light, and what thou speakest is it inwardly from God?" This opened me so that it cut me to the heart; and then I saw clearly we were all wrong. So I sat down in

my pew again, and cried bitterly. And I cried in my spirit to the Lord, "We are all thieves, we are all thieves, we have taken the Scriptures in words and know nothing of them in ourselves." I saw it was the truth and . . . I received the truth in the love of it. And it was opened to me so clear that I had never a tittle in my heart against it; but I desired the Lord that I might be kept in it.[5]

And so Margaret stopped quoting the Scriptures and started living them. She became like Lydia and the other independent women who were allies of Paul and hosts of the earliest churches, as recorded in the Book of Acts. She made her home a hospitality center for the traveling preachers of the early Quaker movement. She coordinated correspondence and handled the finances of the movement in these earliest years. She also maintained regular meetings for worship at Swarthmoor Hall.

Judge Fell died in 1658 and the legal protection he was able to provide the movement in his vicinity began to erode. In 1660, monarchy and a state-sponsored church were restored, and Friends encountered more serious, systemic persecution. Fearing Quakers as political subversives, Parliament passed the Quaker Act in 1663, banning Quaker meetings of five or more. Margaret was arrested for persisting in hosting Quaker worship in her home. At her trial, the judge demanded that she swear an oath of allegiance to the government, knowing that as a Quaker she would refuse to swear any oath. When Margaret refused, she was committed to indefinite imprisonment. In the legal language of the day, she was no longer "under the King's protection": her rights as a subject of the realm were suspended. But she later wrote of that terrible moment, "The great God of heaven and earth supported my spirit under this severe sentence, [so] I was not terrified but gave this answer to Judge Turner . . . 'Although I am out of the King's protection, I am not out of the protection of the Almighty God.'"[6] She spent the next four years imprisoned at Lancaster Castle.

Like George, Margaret used the time well. She wrote letters to King Charles, working for an end to the persecution of Friends. She also wrote various published tracts. The most significant of these was *Women's Speaking Justified,* published in 1666. It was her defense of Christ's authority to speak and lead through women as well as men. Today it is considered to be one of the great proto-feminist tracts. Margaret and other early Friends reread New Testament epistles that people then assumed (as many still do today) clearly instructed women to keep quiet. For example, she refers to 1 Corinthians 14:34: "Let your women keep silence . . . it is not permitted unto them to speak . . . as saith the Law." She responds, "But where Women are led by the Spirit of God, they are not under the Law, for Christ in the Male and in the Female are one; and where he is made manifest in Male and Female, he may speak, for 'he is the end of the Law for righteousness [sake]'" (see Romans 10:4).[7]

There is insightful scholarship in *Women's Speaking Justified.* But the primary source of Fell's insights was the *experience* she and other early Quaker women had of the Spirit speaking and acting through them. They answered the radical call to speak up and speak out in a culture that often persecuted women who got out of line. And as they lived into a radical faith, as they lived the crisis, they reread Scripture and heard new things.

I'll close with one more story, of a lesser known early Quaker prophet, **Ann Audland**. She and her husband John were in their early 20s and among the thousands of Seekers who responded to George Fox's preaching around northern England in May and June of 1652. That was the ground-zero moment when the Quaker movement became a recognizable phenomenon. Ann and John Audland became part of the Valiant Sixty. John Audland paired up with his friend John Camm. In 1654, they invaded Bristol with the Quaker message. Bristol was the second largest city in England at that time, and a hotbed of seeking groups. The two Johns, Camm and Audland, had spectacular success there. (Another story of John Camm is the subject of Chapter 9.)

Ann Audland teamed up with Mabel Camm, wife of John, and they began their own itinerant ministry. They were preaching in the streets of the Oxfordshire town of Banbury in 1655 when Ann was physically assaulted in the street by some ruffians. She later told the local parish priest that this violence was a symptom of his spiritual influence. For this and other provocative statements, she was arrested and charged with blasphemy (we will return to Ann's "blasphemy" in Chapter 12). Someone posted bail for her and she resumed preaching around the area for some months before her trial. Many were convinced and local meetings were started.

But the local establishment was outraged by "that prating woman Audland." It was reported that those who listened to her quaked and foamed at the mouth. Some said she was a witch and should be burned. But the judge at her trial was a more moderate man. He offered to free her if she would swear to stop causing trouble. But of course Ann could neither swear an oath nor desist from preaching. So she spent eight months in prison, kept in an underground cell that "did stink sorely; besides frogs and toads did crawl in," as she later wrote.

Like George Fox at Derby, Ann took imprisonment not as defeat but an opportunity to lay siege to the town of Banbury with the truth. Other Quaker leaders converged there to nurture newly convinced Friends, to agitate among local sympathizers, and to protest Ann's imprisonment.

Richard Farnworth was one of them, and he too was imprisoned for his preaching. More seeking people became Friends as he preached through the grate in his prison window. As her time in prison wore on, Ann Audland wrote to Margaret Fell, saying, "This is indeed a place of joy, and my soul doth rejoice in the Lord. I continue a prisoner in Banbury, but I witness freedom in the Lord."[8]

# 2

## THE PASSION OF JAMES PARNELL

JAMES PARNELL WAS a teenage Quaker street preacher. He was 18 years old and living in northern England in 1653 when he was convinced by George Fox's message. By the next year, he was traveling in ministry around the county of Essex, northeast of London. His prophetic street preaching convinced many Seekers around Colchester, which quickly became a hotbed of the Quaker movement. But not everyone was convinced by this 19-year-old Quaker phenom. One day he was attacked in the street by an angry mob. A local butcher struck him with a barrel stave and knocked him to the ground, saying, "Take that for Jesus Christ's sake." Parnell looked up, saying "Friend, I do receive it for Jesus Christ's sake."[9]

The difference between the butcher's faith and Parnell's is the difference the Quaker movement made for many Seekers at that time. For more than a century, the Protestant Reformation had seen people violently defending one doctrine against another, fighting wars to promote one church over another. England had just ended a bloody civil war, fought partly over religious questions. The butcher was locked into that mindset: defending Jesus, striking a blow for Christ, beating false doctrine to the ground. "Take that for Jesus Christ's sake."

James Parnell understood something deeper. Jesus didn't defend himself. We don't need to defend him either. The point of the gospel is to immerse ourselves in his story and make it our own story in some way. We do that as we learn to let his Spirit breathe through us, to speak through our words and actions. That's a powerful shift in consciousness—it's not so much *about* Christ as *in* Christ. It's not only faith *in* Jesus, but sharing the faith *of* Jesus. That's the faith that empowered James Parnell to look up from the pavement and say, "Friend, I do receive it for Jesus Christ's sake."

Tragically, James Parnell went still further in sharing the faith—and fate—of Jesus. Soon after that incident and some others, he was arrested for causing riots. He was imprisoned at Colchester Castle. From there, he wrote a letter to the new Friends around Essex that he had convinced:

> As I had a time to preach the Truth amongst you, to the convincement of many, so also now I have a time to seal the same with patient suffering in the bonds of the gospel, that you may see that it is no other but what we are made able and willing to seal with patient suffering, yea, with our blood, if we are called to it . . . . Be willing that self shall suffer for the Truth, and not the Truth for the self.[10]

Parnell was kept there and mistreated until he died in April 1656—the first martyr of the Quaker movement. The passion of Jesus became the passion of James Parnell, and of many more to come. More than 450 Friends died under persecution in England and Wales before they were finally granted religious freedom in 1689. Our little Quaker niche in the world was bought at a dear price.

But our gain was not just about the survival of a little religious denomination, another religious option for people to select from a long menu in this country. The radical Christian faith of early Friends like James Parnell pioneered what today we call nonviolent direct action. Nonviolent direct action is where we stand resolutely together for some principle of love, truth, justice, or equality, and let others respond as they will.

When you think about it, that's what Jesus did. But over the centuries, church doctrine completely encased the death of Jesus in the doctrine of atonement, the teaching that Jesus died for our sins. This other meaning of his life and death was lost. It took Gandhi, on the other side of the planet, to rediscover the principles of nonviolent direct action. Gandhi said that he developed them in part from reading the Sermon on the Mount. It's ironic that we modern Quakers had to learn nonviolent direct action all over again from Gandhi, when it's there so strongly in our own deep history.

Of course, Martin Luther King is the towering figure of nonviolent direct action in our time and in this country. A Baptist preacher, King lived and preached the message. He relied on others for the strategies of the movement, in particular the African American Quaker Bayard Rustin. But King himself is the iconic figure because he lived the nonviolent struggle not as a technique for social change, but as he made the passion of Jesus his own passion. That's clear from end to end of his 13 years leading the civil rights movement. As one of his biographers summarized, he was bearing the cross.[11]

When we make the passion of Jesus our passion, in whatever degree, we will have a powerful effect on others. Whether the conversion is to Christ or to the cause of peace and justice, the principle is the same. I don't know if that butcher in the streets of Colchester that day was converted. Our nonviolent witness can't guarantee results. But we do know that another young man named Stephen Crisp was among the onlookers at that scene in the street. He's the one who told the story, years later. Crisp became an important leader in the Quaker movement around Colchester for many years to come. He caught the contagion of Quakerism, the contagion of a radical Christian faith, from James Parnell that day. I guess that's another way we can describe the difference between the butcher's faith and James Parnell's. The butcher had been taught the faith in Jesus. James Parnell had caught the faith of Jesus. He had all the symptoms. He was contagious.

Of course, the faith of Jesus isn't all about getting beaten up or spending time in jail. The more common, everyday symptoms include "love, joy, peace, patience, kindness, generosity, faithfulness, gentleness, and self-control." Paul called these symptoms "the fruit of the Spirit" (Gal. 5:22-23). Big, dramatic moments like the story of James Parnell are built out of small, everyday moments, as the Spirit steadily bears fruit in our lives.

# 3

---

## JOHN BURNYEAT AND CUMBERLAND FRIENDS:
## CROSSING THE RED SEA IN 1653

A S WE HAVE seen, biblical stories framed the way early Friends understood the call to radical faithfulness. And as they answered that call, it also deepened their reading of Scripture. Another good example is John Burnyeat's story of Quaker beginnings in Cumberland, in the far north of England. Burnyeat was a 22-year-old farmer there when George Fox and other Quaker prophets arrived in 1653. He and a group of others were convinced of the Quaker message. They began to meet for worship and to adopt Quaker plainness of speech and dress. Quaker convincement turned these people inside out and their world upside down. The light in their consciences exposed their most intimate thoughts and motives. Burnyeat describes it with an endless stream of biblical images: "The day of the Lord that makes desolate had overtaken us, and the fire and sword that Christ brings upon the earth, by which he takes away peace, had reached us."[12]

Burnyeat, like many other early Friends, uses the Israelite exodus from bondage in Egypt as a central paradigm for interpreting this harrowing passage in the Spirit. He writes, "Deep were our groanings and our cries unto the Lord, which reached unto him." Here Burnyeat echoes the passage in Exodus 2 that says that under the hardship of Egyptian slavery, the Israelites groaned under their bondage and cried out. Verses 22 and 23 of Exodus 2 read, "Out of the slavery their cry for help rose up to God. God heard their groanings and God remembered his covenant with Abraham, Isaac, and Jacob" (2:23-24).[13]

Quaker worship in these first years was full of groaning and sighing. (We're fortunate that we were dubbed with the nickname "Quakers" and not "Groaners.") They believed that they needed to vocalize their spiritual captivity as part of the process of liberation. Like their quaking, it was an embodied, nonverbal form of prayer that drew God into the struggle. This practice is also mentioned in Romans 8, where Paul refers to sighing or groaning in early Christian worship. The Spirit groans in us with sighs too deep for words, a groaning that is also in solidarity with the rest of creation. Early Friends groaned in solidarity with the Israelite slaves, the early Christians, the rest of creation, and the Spirit of God in them.

But help was slow in coming. "Our hearts were unstable, like water—the waves going over our heads." (In Chapter 7 we will hear Fox use this image in an early epistle to Friends.) God was weaning them of all the comfort and help they thought they could draw from the world: "We began to forsake all on both hands, seeing the emptiness of all, the glory, vanity, and pleasure of the world *and* the dead image of profession [religious doctrine]." To make matters worse, as they met more often, they were mocked and abused by their neighbors, family, and friends. And when they witnessed their new faith, local church members accused them of heresy for following a light within. Burnyeat writes,

> In this weak state we were beset on every hand, and greatly distressed, tossed, and afflicted, as poor Israel were, when the sea was before them, and the Egyptians behind—and their hope so little, that they looked for nothing but death.

We will return later to the passage in Exodus Burnyeat refers to here. But first, let's continue his story a bit further. He writes that their problem was that they had not yet found "true striving," which is "out of self." Fortunately, more Quaker ministers passed through and gave them further instruction in Quaker waiting worship. As he describes it, the ministers came to "direct us *in what* to wait, and *how* to stand still, *out* of our own thoughts and self-strivings, *in the light* that doth discover." Perhaps there was more technique to the early Quaker practice of standing still in the light than we know of today.

This counsel began to help them. He writes, "We got to some degree of staidness in our minds, which before had been as the troubled sea, and a hope began to appear in us; and we met together often, and waited to see the salvation of God . . . the wonderful power from on high was revealed among us." As they met more often, "Great dread and trembling fell upon many, and the very Chains of Death was broken . . . the Prisoners of hope began to come forth."

And as they grew stronger, they also grew bolder in their witness. They began to draw others away from the local clergy and to Christ's direct teaching. As Burnyeat puts it, the Lamb and his followers struck at the kingdom of the Beast, "which made him begin to rage, and stir up his Instruments to oppose the Lord's Work . . . . The Beast and his followers began to war, and whipping, and scourging, and prisoning, and spoiling of Goods . . . slandering the way of Truth . . . calling his Light natural, insufficient, [a] false Guide."

Burnyeat uses Lamb's War imagery here. The first generation of Friends drew this from the Book of Revelation, to describe their liberation struggle against the coercive religion of the state-sponsored church. The Lamb's War begins as an inward struggle, then becomes an outward struggle. The community enters into nonviolent direct action against the powers that had held them in spiritual captivity. We'll return to the Lamb's War later, especially in Chapter 8.

But for now, let us focus on Burnyeat's key description of their condition, both before and after the Quaker "spiritual directors," we might call them, arrived. It's a powerful paradigm of answering the call to radical faithfulness—in our spiritual practice, in our lives of personal integrity, and in our wider witness in the world.

He compares their experience to that of the Israelites on the banks of the Red Sea. You may recall that when the Pharaoh finally released the Israelites, they started out into the wilderness. But then Pharaoh changed his mind and sent an army of chariots into the wilderness after them. We pick up the story in the 10th verse of Exodus 14:

> As Pharaoh drew near, the Israelites looked back and there were the Egyptians advancing on them. In great fear the Israelites cried out to the Lord. They said to Moses, "Was it because there were no graves in Egypt that you have taken us away to die in the wilderness? What have you done to us, bringing us out of Egypt? Is this not the very thing we told you in Egypt, 'Let us alone and let us serve the Egyptians'? For it would have been better for us to serve the Egyptians than to die in the wilderness."

> But Moses said to the people, "Do not be afraid, stand firm, and see the deliverance that the Lord will accomplish for you today; for the Egyptians whom you see today you shall never see again. The Lord will fight for you, and you have only to keep still."

> Then the Lord said to Moses, "Why do you cry out to me? Tell the Israelites to go forward. But you lift up your staff, and stretch out your hand over the sea and divide it, that the Israelites may go into the sea on dry ground."

The Israelite complaints to Moses reveal that sarcasm is not a modern invention. "Was it because there were no graves in Egypt that you have taken us away to die in the wilderness?" Ancient Egypt was a deeply *necrophilic* empire. They utilized slave labor to build the pyramids, monumental tombs for the Pharaohs; and they developed advanced techniques of mummification.

But there's also great human truth in this complaint. Any of us on the path of liberation from addiction or other forms of human bondage will sometimes look back fondly on that life and dearly long to return to it. And that's the acute moment that Burnyeat describes in himself and his Friends. They were becoming local pariahs, facing the rejection and hostility of family, friends, neighbors, employers—the Egyptian chariots bearing down behind them.

The sea in front of them was their impasse in worship. They hadn't found the place to stand, how to stand still out of their own thoughts and wills, where the light reveals all and gives strength to make changes and face opposition. That clearly relates to Moses' answer to his people: "Don't be afraid, *stand firm*, and see the deliverance that the Lord will accomplish for you today; for the Egyptians whom you see today you shall never see again. The Lord will fight for you, and *you have only to keep still*." The Lamb's War begins and proceeds as we stand still and see God's deliverance, where we let the Lord do the fighting and striving for us.

Moses began learning that great truth that day he stood still in front of the burning bush and answered his call to radical faithfulness. Every step of the way, Moses had let the Lord's power work through him; now, he tried to teach this lesson to his people.

The paradox of this story, of course, is that just as Moses imparted this crucial truth, God snapped at Moses, "Why do you cry out to me? Tell the Israelites to go forward. But you lift up your staff, and stretch out your hand over the sea and divide it, that the Israelites may go into the sea on dry ground."

There's a powerful paradox here: somehow, *standing still is also the way forward*. Resting from our own ideas and efforts reveals what we really need to do. This is the lesson we learn at every step of our own path, from inward transformation, to changing our own personal lifestyle choices, to our social witness in the world.

It is worth noting that early Friends didn't bother themselves with our modern questions like, did Moses really part the waters of the Red Sea, so the Israelites could walk through? Those historical-critical questions were not yet on their horizon in the mid-17<sup>th</sup> century. But early Friends read the Bible not so much literally as *existentially*. They saw these stories replayed in their own struggles as individuals and as a people. And out of their own struggles, they understood and interconnected the biblical stories at a deeper level.

The story of crossing the Red Sea can speak to our own personal experience of answering the call to radical faithfulness. But primarily, it's the story of *the birth of a people*, out of captivity, into a shared liberation. The Hebrew word for Egypt, *Mitzrayim*, has its root in the Hebrew verb *myitz*, to squeeze, to press. Rabbi Arthur Waskow translates the word for Egypt, *Mitzrayim,* as "a tight and narrow place."[14] Israel was squeezed, oppressed by enslavement by its Egyptian captors. Passing out of Egypt, that narrow place, through the birth waters of the Red Sea, was the birth of a people—a radically new kind of people, like nothing the world had seen.

Likewise, early Friends passed out of the spiritual captivity of a state-sponsored Church, ruled by an enfranchised clerical class, teaching a narrow, creedal faith. They passed through the harrowing experience of the light's unsparing revelation, into a new sense of freedom and empowerment. It was the birth of a new people, another people like nothing the world had seen.

But we modern Friends cannot simply inherit that peoplehood. We too must pass through our own Red Sea, our own baptism of the Spirit, our own rebirth as a people. And in that process, we too can learn from the words of Moses and find their meaning in our own circumstances. Those words still call to us today: "Don't be afraid, stand firm, and see the deliverance that the Lord will accomplish for you today . . . . The Lord will fight for you, and you have only to keep still." And as we stand more resolutely in that moment of crisis, the way forward appears. We find ourselves entering the sea on solid ground. We find ourselves on our way out of the necrophilic empire of our own times, and into a radically new life.

# 4

## SARAH JONES, SARAH BLACKBOROW, AND FRANCIS HOWGILL: LEARNING TO STAY AT HOME WITH JACOB

I GREW UP in a large, mildly liberal pastoral Friends meeting in Indianapolis. I went to Sunday school most Sundays and heard various stories from the Bible. I just let them wash over me. I wasn't pushed to believe anything in particular. The stories were told mainly as good moral lessons or tales of heroic faith. I must admit, I didn't take any of it too seriously. Later, I was a student at Indiana University, a zoology major and not involved with any church or meeting. But much to my surprise, early in my sophomore year, I received a distinct calling to be a minister. So I started taking some courses in religion. One of the first was an Old Testament survey course.

That term, I quickly realized that the Bible is not a compendium of morality tales. The scales really fell from my eyes when I read the cycle of Jacob stories in Genesis. Jacob, the son of Isaac and Rebecca, the grandson of Abraham and Sarah, is not exactly a hero or a moral exemplar. He's an antihero and a trickster. In fact, the whole Jacob cycle has just about everyone playing some kind of trick on someone else. My love of the Bible began when I read the Jacob cycle in Genesis and realized that something more interesting than fairy tales and morality plays is going on here.

I would enjoy savoring the whole Jacob story with you. But for our present purposes, I'll just point out that Jacob is a twin. As you may recall, his brother Esau was first out of Rebecca's womb, with Jacob right behind, holding onto his heel. What an image of sibling rivalry! Esau grows up to be a man of the field, a hunter. Their father Isaac is fond of Esau because he puts meat on the table. Jacob is a more retiring personality, hanging around the tents with their mother, Rebecca, who favors him. And apparently Jacob makes a really delicious lentil stew. (Maybe there's a vegetarian level to this story.)

Speaking of different interpretations, I have enjoyed and learned from New England Friend Peterson Toscano's dramatic presentation of Jacob and his son Joseph as gender nonconforming characters of the Bible.[15] . I'll never see Jacob or Joseph the same way. The Genesis stories are so richly archetypal, they can be read in many different ways, depending on what experiences we bring to them. But my concern in this chapter is with how early Friends read the story out of their own experience, and what we might learn from them.

You may recall that Jacob twice tricks Esau, first out of the birthright and then out of their father's blessing. First, when Esau is famished from hunting, he trades his birthright for a bowl of Jacob's tempting lentil stew. And later, their mother Rebecca schemes with Jacob to trick old, blind Isaac into blessing Jacob instead of the firstborn Esau. There is much more to the Jacob story. But for our purposes, let's stop here and see how early Friends read that story out of their own experience. It has bearing on the call to radical faithfulness.

Jacob shows up early in the Quaker saga, in an epistle by **Sarah Jones**. We don't know much about her. We're not even sure she became a Quaker. But she published a letter to like-minded Seekers in 1650, before the Quaker movement took form. This letter contains spiritual counsel very similar to what George Fox was writing around the same time. Before we look at an excerpt from that letter, it's important to say something about the highly charged historical moment when it was written.

The English Civil War, from 1643 to 1648, was a war to decide the future of both politics and religion in England. Many joined in Parliament's battle against King Charles, some with hopes not just for reform but for nothing less than the kingdom of heaven on earth. Early during the war, both censorship of the press and forced parish church attendance were suspended. All sorts of radical ideas in politics and religion found their way into print, and a variety of new, experimental churches and worship groups sprouted up without state repression.

Charles was finally defeated in 1648. He was tried for treason and beheaded at the beginning of 1649. Radical hopes ran at fever pitch. Some looked for greater religious freedom and an expanded electoral franchise; others for Christ to arrive as England's new king. But soon many of these most radical spirits began to despair, as they watched Puritan forces in Parliament and the army assert a more conservative control. By 1650, the hopes that had loomed so close began to recede. Radicals felt tricked by the powers that had promised so much during the war. It was something like what many of us felt at the end of the 1960s in this country, around the time I was first encountering Jacob the trickster.

During the Civil War, many of the most radical spirits had dropped out of all the churches, waiting for some new revelation, for the emergence of a new kind of church for new times. They were called Seekers, and they were among the most disillusioned in 1650. Some were swept up in the outburst of Ranterism in 1649-50. It's hard to give a brief definition of the Ranters that's also adequate. They were less a movement than a spontaneous rebellion from Puritan morality and the new Puritan establishment. Leading Ranter writers were deeply religious people, some of them ministers. But they wrote that light and darkness, good and evil, amount to the same thing. One of them wrote that if something seems sinful to you, you should just keep doing until it feels right. The Ranter outburst sent the Puritan regime into a moral panic. Parliament passed a Blasphemy Act in August 1650 to suppress the phenomenon with a six-month prison sentence for heresy.[16] (The authorities in Derby used the Act to imprison George Fox the following October, as mentioned in Chapter 1. His teaching of perfection was mistaken for a Ranter indifference to sin.)

Sarah Jones's letter appears to be written to Seekers who were mourning, but not ranting. She writes to them as people who have received some powerful revelations from God but now feel lost. She writes,

> Dear Lambs, whom the Father hath visited with his eternal love, this is the Message of the Lord unto you . . . sink down into the eternal word, and rest there . . . sink down into the measure of life that ye have received . . . keep in that which is pure, which is the eternal word of the Lord . . . look not at your own weakness, but look at him who is calling you in his eternal love, who will make the weak strong, and will pull down the mighty from their seat . . . stand still and see the salvation of God, which is the light of his Covenant. . . .
>
> So cease thy mourning, thou weeping babe, that mourns in secret for manifestations from thy beloved, as thou hast had in dayes past; for I can testifie unto thee by experience . . . that he is bringing thee nearer him . . . if thou be willing and obedient to live at home with *Jacob*, which is daily to retire thy mind; though the gadding, hunting *Esau* persecutes thee for it, thou shalt receive the blessing in which all happiness and felicity doth consist for evermore. For *Esau* went to hunt abroad, when the blessing was to be received at home. Therefore come down, come down to the Word of his patience, which is nigh in your hearts. . . . For oh, the glorious day of the Lord hasteth to be revealed to those who are kept faithful in his Word.[17]

Sarah Jones's letter probably circulated among the networks of Seekers that would soon coalesce into the Quaker movement. These men and women were learning how to sink down, to stand still, to wait where the power is to be found. They no longer waited *for* Parliament or the army to fulfill their promises. They began waiting *upon* the Lord, where the power is. And that power would soon break out in their experience, in their bodies, and in their revolutionary witness.

Sarah Jones found the ancient story of Jacob and Esau resonant with her own experience. She and many other Seekers had been like Esau, hunting abroad for the next great teacher, the next book of spiritual wisdom, or waiting on the next promising development in the political drama around them. It wore them down, to the point of despair, like Esau ready to sell his birthright. But now they were becoming more like Jacob, retiring the mind from its hunting, sinking down to the source within, where they found true wisdom and renewed strength.

Eight years later, in 1658, the London Quaker Sarah Blackborow made the same point when she chided Seekers who still had not made that crucial turn:

> Wisdom hath uttered forth her voice to you, but the eye and ear which is abroad, waiting upon a sound of words without you, is that which keeps you from your Teacher within you; and this is the reason that in all your seekings you have found nothing; such as your seeking is, such is your finding.[18]

Outward seeking leads in all directions, with only fleeting rewards and shards of wisdom: "Such as your seeking is, such is your finding." Blackborow doesn't make use of the Jacob-Esau typology, but her point is the same that we found in Sarah Jones's epistle.

**Francis Howgill** records his own seeking journey in *The Inheritance of Jacob Discovered* (1655). He tells how he bounced during the war from church to church, group to group, teacher to teacher. He eventually became a leading preacher among a network of Seekers in Westmorland, in northern England.

But he still lacked the spiritual power he sought. He was 34 years old when he and about a thousand other Seekers heard George Fox preach on Firbank Fell, Westmorland in June 1652. Three years later, in *The Inheritance of Jacob Discovered*, Howgill counseled other Seekers,

> [T]herefore all honest-hearted [ones], who travel and are weary and have found no rest for your souls, I say unto you . . . lie not groveling in the earth; nor seek to know God in your fallen wisdom, for the well is deep, and if you know nothing but the old wisdom . . . you cannot come to one drop of the living water . . . . Return home again . . . you are further off in running out, and seeking in your earthly wisdom and comprehension, than you were before.[19]

Howgill discovered Jacob's inheritance by returning "home" and digging deeper to find the living water, his inward teacher. He alludes here to Jacob's well, where Jesus and the Samaritan woman talked about living water (John 4; see also Gen. 33:18-20; 48:22; Josh. 24:32). Howgill became one of the key leaders of the Quaker movement. He and Edward Burrough had enormous success in spreading the movement to London in 1654, guiding thousands of Seekers to Jacob's well.

We are finding again and again that early Friends reread the Bible in light of their own experience, a deep passage through crisis and despair—a despair of themselves and a despair of the religious and political crisis of their times. They understood their personal crisis and the crisis of their times as one crisis.

These Seekers turned Quakers discovered the "inheritance of Jacob," a counterintuitive truth. Sinking down is counterintuitive when you already feel yourself sinking into despair and you're grasping at straws. Standing still in the light is counterintuitive when you want to run away and find help somewhere else. Retiring the mind is counterintuitive when you're sure that the answer is just one more book, one more Google search away. This counter-intuitive, paradoxical truth resonated for early Friends with the story of Jacob, the trickster. It's the same truth that John Burnyeat and his friends found in the Exodus story: standing still becomes the way forward when there's no way forward.

But it's worth noting that the Ranters inadvertently played an important part in this breakthrough. Many Seekers passed through at least a brief ranting phase on their way to becoming Quakers. Isaac Penington is one. He wrote some rather colorful tracts in 1650, eight years before his Quaker convincement. But as long as you have your moral glasses fixed firmly on your nose, you'll see only your preconceived notions of good. And the good gets in the way of God. That's where we encounter the moral ambiguity of Jacob the trickster. Only by suffering through the eclipse of the ego, where our moral commitments are invested, can we encounter the divine as a living reality¾sometimes a scary reality.

Once that encounter has taken place, a new moral sense can develop, at a higher level of integration. That's part of the Jacob story as well. Remember that Jacob the trickster eventually had to confront his past, when he wrestled all night with an angel. By dawn, he was a new man with a new identity: Israel, the father of a new people (Gen. 32). But if he hadn't played the trickster first, he might still have been in the tents with his mother.

Even George Fox had some good things to say for the Ranters. He wrote that they had had some great revelations, but had "fled the cross." That is, they didn't stand still in that place where real transformation takes place. They "went a little bit crazy," as they say in country-western songs.

All through the 1650s, when Quakers were at their most confrontational and revolutionary, the Puritans mistook them for Ranters. They seemed more than "a little bit crazy." But while Ranters recanted and slinked back home after spending time in England's miserable jails, Quakers just got stronger, as we've seen in previous chapters. The Lamb's War—the Quaker nonviolent campaign in steeplehouses, marketplaces, and the streets across England—was indeed relentlessly jarring. It was an enormous release of energies not simply from the lower classes of society, but from a place deep within people of various classes.

The Lamb's War was a grassroots social revolution of men and women answering the call to radical faithfulness. It was defeated in its larger aims for social transformation. But it produced a Religious Society of Friends that still pursues the vision in various more rational ways. Our modern Quaker faith and practice were generated largely from the experiments and discoveries of that early, dynamic movement. But the revolutionary meaning of it all evaporated over time. We look back on it simply as the beginnings of our beloved Religious Society of Friends. (For more about the Lamb's War, see my 1995 book, *The Covenant Crucified: Quakers and the Rise of Capitalism*. For many more stories of Seekers and Ranters becoming Quakers, see my 2000 book, *Seekers Found: Atonement in Early Quaker Experience*.)

But Jacob the trickster still lurks among us. In the last century, Quakers were among the early allies of Gandhi and Martin Luther King. Even though we no longer understood our Quaker beginnings in revolutionary terms, Gandhi's and King's nonviolent campaigns resonated with the deep structures of our spiritual tradition. Richard Gregg, the son of a Congregationalist minister, brought Gandhi's teachings to America in 1934 and started teaching at Pendle Hill that same year. His 1935 book, *The Power of Nonviolence*, described nonviolent action as "moral Jiu-Jitsu." He explained how nonviolent resisters throw oppressors off guard and make them unsure of their position by using moral power to "convert the opponent, to change his understanding and his sense of values. [20] Gregg's influence on the American civil rights movement and on future generations of Quaker activists is well documented. But the power of nonviolent direct action is right there in our own deep history.

Perhaps with the moral jujitsu of nonviolent resistance, we catch sight of Jacob the trickster reappearing. But if we utilize nonviolent action simply as a technique for social change, it will remain only a moral jujitsu. The greater power that sustained early Friends was a *spiritual* jujitsu, an experience that turns us inside out and our world upside down. It's the counterintuitive wisdom we learn by spending time "at home" with Jacob.

# 5

## GEORGE FOX TO HIS PARENTS: "YOU HAVE NO TIME BUT THIS PRESENT TIME"

GEORGE FOX WROTE to his parents, back home in Fenny Drayton in the English Midlands, in 1652, the year the Quaker movement took off as a recognizable phenomenon. Fox, 28 years old, was moving quickly around the North of England, gathering large groups of Seekers into the movement. But he was also suffering severe beatings by hostile mobs for what he was saying. Fox may have written to his parents thinking that he might not survive these attacks much longer. Yet this brief letter is full of joy and hope.

Not many parents have received a letter like this one. Fox writes in one passage:

> Oh! Be faithful! Look not back, nor be too forward, further than you have attained; for you have no time, but this present time: therefore prize your time for your souls' sake. And so grow up in that which is pure, and keep to the oneness; then shall my joy be full. So fare you well!

Not many sons or daughters urge their parents to "grow up." But young George is inviting his parents to grow up in the Spirit, in the fullness of time, which is the present time. Don't hearken back to things past, he urges, but also don't be too forward, beyond where you really are now: there *is* no time but his present time, so prize this time. This is particularly striking. We spend so much time dwelling on the past, longingly or with regret; or having big ideas about the future, in hope or dread. But the past and the future do not exist. We have only the present; this is the time to cherish.

Some years ago, I did extensive research on the early Seekers and other religious and political radicals and how they converged in the Quaker movement. I discovered that there were two main kinds of Seekers. Some were seeking a way back to the purity and power of the New Testament Church. The whole Protestant Reformation had been about getting back to "primitive Christianity revived," as William Penn put it. Different Protestant churches were different chapter-and-verse reconstructions of early Christian faith and practice. Each claimed to be the right one. They debated and even went to war over these differences. Finally, by the end of the Reformation, these Seekers concluded that the only way back was not by the letter of Scripture, but by a fresh pouring out of the Spirit, just as the Pentecost had gathered the church in the first place. One could say that this first kind of Seeker was conservative, but driven to radical conclusions.

But there were other Seekers who asked, why would God take us back to a church that corrupted so soon after it started? They believed that the church had started going off the rails by the end of the first century. No, they concluded, God isn't taking us backward but forward, into a new age of the Spirit, a new age just about to dawn. They had big ideas about what this new age would be like. This second kind of Seeker was progressive, in an early modern form. They viewed each age of history coming to a higher revelation, a clearer vision of truth, and an advance of the human condition. But their dreams were far ahead of where they were standing in the present.[21]

The Quaker movement pulled both of these kinds of Seekers together, from their backward longing and their forward striving, into the present.

They stopped waiting *for* the Lord to bring back the Pentecost or to bring on the new age. They started waiting *upon* the Lord in the present. They became present to the Presence of God in the present moment. The called their silent worship waiting upon the Lord, a way of becoming present.

I wonder if George found something like the Seeker divergence in his parents. Perhaps one of them tended to look backward to "the good old days," while the other looked forward to better things to come.

I have traveled widely among Friends over the years, and I have found these two tendencies in every meeting I've been part of. Some of us look backward longingly to things about the life of the meeting we liked better in the past. Others of us strain forward, for the meeting to become something new and better, something more faithful, more successful by some standard or another. Most of us are some combination of those two. And in the meetings where I've been a pastor, I always find myself in the middle. I share some of the feelings and aspirations of both groups, and I try to keep those two motivations from pulling the meeting apart.

But I also keep in mind George Fox's advice. We have no time but the present time. Therefore, let us prize our time together, for our own sakes and for the sake of the meeting. To "prize" something can have two meanings. Most often, we mean that we value something, take it seriously, protect it. But it can also mean opening it up. We usually say we *pry* something open, though the older usage is to *prize* something open.

That is what we do when we come together in Quaker worship. We prize our time together. We wait upon the Lord; we wait in the quiet. And if we are patient, the present will open up to us; the Lord will reveal something to us that we don't notice when we're busy, when we're talking or reading, working or playing. We also don't notice it when we long for the past or grasp for the future.

But it's also true that by prizing the present time together, we gain insight in how to move forward together. Moving forward into the future is not just about doing new things: it often includes taking the best from the past. Recycling and repurposing can sometimes be more successful than trying to invent something new. When we are grounded in the present, the past and the future are not a contradiction but a conversation that unfolds among us. So let us prize this time together—it's all we've got.

# 6

## GEORGE FOUGHT THE BATTLE OF JERICHO: KENDAL, 1652

IN CHAPTER 1, I noted how George Fox's year of imprisonment at Derby, England radicalized his message and his methods. When he was finally released in late 1651, he felt like a lion coming out of its den among the beasts of the forest. Fox's ministry indeed became more confrontational after Derby than it had been before. While he was still in prison at Derby, he received teaching from the Lord that when he was freed, he was to enter "steeple-houses" (parish church buildings) to draw people out, as the apostles had entered synagogues to draw people out.[22] And from the stories of Paul in Acts, he knew this meant trouble—conflict, spontaneous outbursts of violence, arrests and imprisonments. I also noted in Chapter 1 that Fox's encounters with James Nayler and other radicals in West Yorkshire at the end of 1651 added still more social edge to his ministry. We'll devote more attention to James Nayler in Chapter 8.

But in this chapter, I want to look at one of my favorite episodes in Fox's *Journal,* from the pivotal year of 1652. Fox passed through the northern market town of Kendal one day that summer or autumn. He describes the event thus:

And so I returned back into Westmorland again and spoke through Kendal upon a market day. I had silver in my pocket and was moved to throw it out amongst the people as I was going up the street before I spoke, and my life was offered up amongst them and the mighty power of the Lord was seen in preserving and the power of the Lord was so mighty and so strong that people flew like chaff before me, and ran into their houses and shops, for fear and terror took hold upon them. I was moved to open my mouth and lift up my voice aloud in the mighty power of the Lord, and to tell them the mighty day of the Lord was coming upon all deceitful merchandise and ways, and to call them all to repentance and a turning to the Lord God, and his spirit within them, for it to teach them and lead them, and tremble before the mighty God of Heaven and earth, for his mighty day was coming; and so passed through the streets. And many people took my part and several were convinced. And when I came to the town's end, I got upon a stump and spoke to the people, and so the people began to fight some for me and some against me, and I went and spoke to them and they parted again. So after a while I passed away without any harm.[23]

Again, as suggested in Chapter 1, early Friends experienced the national crisis of England's uncertain future after the Civil War as a personal, spiritual crisis. At a time when most people wanted to get back to life and business as usual, early Friends kept inducing that sense of crisis through a sustained nonviolent conflict in parish "steeplehouses," streets, and marketplaces across the country. It made them very unpopular.

The scene of that market day in Kendal is one such skirmish in the early Quaker Lamb's War. It suggests how adept Fox had become at inducing that sense of crisis. The streets would have been choked with people buying and selling on this main commercial day of the week. Throwing money out among them was certainly a way to get their attention. It sounds like a riot breaking out—some people diving for pieces of silver, others running to get away from the chaos.

But I suspect that throwing money out among the crowd was not only an attention-getting tactic. It was also a symbolic act in the biblical prophetic tradition. It contrasted with the buying and selling going on all around Fox at that moment. Throwing free money around parallels Fox's emphasis on the free teaching of Christ's light within. Fox always contrasted Christ's free, inward teaching with the tithe-supported, contractual ministry of the clergy in the Church of England, and he does allude here to the teaching of the Spirit.

In addition, Fox and other early Friends often waded into marketplaces around England to condemn what he calls here "deceitful merchandise and ways." In this witness they continued a prophetic tradition going back at least as far as Amos and Hosea in the 8th century BCE (e.g., Hosea 11:7). Town merchants often cheated poor, simple country folk in a variety of ways. For one thing, country people were not adept at bargaining, so they could easily be cheated through misrepresentation and bullying. Early Friends were pioneers in the one-price system of trade and commerce in England: they saw it as a matter of truth-telling and integrity. So they not only refused to recite a creed in church or give an oath in court, they also refused to barter. They set what they felt was a fair price—take it or leave it. It revolutionized commerce in England and helped Friends succeed in business.

But Fox doesn't offer a social critique or advance an economic reform so much as announce "the mighty day of the Lord." He calls people to "tremble before the mighty God of Heaven and earth." He speaks of this terrible day as "coming," but clearly he is inducing that moment of crisis and decision right then and there. He evokes God's awesome presence in that very moment. And that moment of crisis either draws people toward Fox, or drives them away just as vehemently. Fighting even breaks out between these two groups.

Fox ends his description of the incident by remarking that he got out of that one unharmed, and even stopped the crowd from fighting. But it didn't always turn out that way for him in these early years. He was often beaten up, his life threatened, or arrested. He was fortunate to survive these early outbreaks of mob violence, which often took place in parish churches. He was even more fortunate to survive his several imprisonments in lousy, septic jails.

As I remarked at the end of Chapter 2, it's ironic in a way that modern Friends had to relearn nonviolent direct action from Gandhi. There are many demonstrations in early Quaker history of the moral jujitsu that Richard Gregg described when he introduced Gandhian nonviolence to the West in the 1930s. But the early Quaker Lamb's War was more than moral: it struck at a deeper, spiritual level. Even more than that, I would suggest that it was *apocalyptic*. Announcing the Day of the Lord, a day of divine visitation and reckoning, induced a sense of crisis that "ended the world" in the usual ways people understood the world and behaved in it. I mean "apocalyptic" in this experiential, socially engaged sense, not in the usual sense of predictions of the end of the world sometime soon. This was *apocalypse now*.

I discuss this in much greater depth in my first book, *Apocalypse of the Word*.[24] But for our purposes here, I want to explore the deeper biblical resonances of that usage of "Day of the Lord," and the ways in which the Lamb's War invoked the holy war tradition of the Hebrew Scriptures. *Apocalypse? Holy war?* Yikes! You may feel like running away, like the people in Kendal that day. But bear with me, please.

In particular, I will draw on Norman Gottwald's liberationist reconstruction of ancient Israel in his epic study *The Tribes of Yahweh* (1979).[25] I offered a summary of Gottwald's work in the first chapter of my 1995 book, *The Covenant Crucified* (cited earlier), where I developed a social revolutionary understanding of the early Quaker movement.

Gottwald drastically reframes the biblical story of the exodus and conquest of Canaan. He suggests that the exodus of liberated slaves out of slavery in Egypt and through 40 years in the desert was probably not the hundreds of thousands as counted in the Book of Numbers. Rather, a relatively small group emerged from some powerful experience of liberation from slavery in Egypt. They eventually arrived in Canaan with a message about a strange god who was not a force of nature, not the sponsor of a royal dynasty, not a god of fertility, but a god known primarily through the social and historical experience of liberation. These liberated slaves from Egypt began moving among a variety of indigenous Canaanite tribes and clans who were exploited and marginalized by the Canaanite city-states. These walled towns dominated the plains with their chariot armies, so the marginalized resistance groups subsisted mainly in the hills where the chariots couldn't go.

The Israelites began interconnecting these diverse Canaanite groups and radicalized them with the theology of this strange god, Yahweh. Early Yahwism confirmed a traditional tribal, decentralized village society over and against the centralized royal-military-priestly establishments of the city-states. As they made this radical conversion, these groups were no longer Canaanite but Israelite. An Israelite confederation of tribes grew and began moving down from the hills and onto the plains. They gradually isolated the Canaanite walled fortress towns.

Gottwald reads the story of the fall of Jericho in Joshua 6 as a symbolic representation of the way this liberation process worked in many cases. As the story is told, Israelite spies infiltrated Jericho and found an ally in the prostitute Rahab. Rahab may be a historical figure, but she probably stands as a collective representation of women who were forced by debt into slavery and prostitution in the Canaanite social system. Rahab informed the spies that the whole town was in dread of the Israelites. She told them, "There is no courage left in any of us because of you. Yahweh your God is indeed God of heaven above and on earth below" (Joshua 2:11).

So, as the story continues, the Israelites came and marched around the walls of the city for seven days, blowing ram's horns (rather unnerving to those on the inside, we might imagine). On the seventh day, the Sabbath, they let out a great shout. That shout probably included something about the "day of the Lord," the "day of Yahweh." Gottwald believes "the day of Yahweh" was a rallying-cry in the Israelite liberation struggle. It was day of liberation that interrupted the timeless cycles of fertility religion that had been subsumed by Canaanite priests and kings to serve as forms of social control and economic exploitation.

The day of the Lord was thus a *crisis*, a decisive moment, breaking into the static world of the Canaanite regime. At this moment the walls "came a-tumblin' down," as the old spiritual puts it. The way the story is told, the walls were breached by the sheer "power of the Lord." But Gottwald suggests that they were breached *from within* by groups that were ready to join the Israelite confederation. It was no less the "power of the Lord," but it was the power of liberating faith working through people's hearts. It's a moment similar to the one we explored in Chapter 3, where the Israelites stood still and let the Lord fight for them on the banks of the Red Sea.

Now, Gottwald doesn't try to portray Israelite holy war as consistently nonviolent. But he argues persuasively that the Canaanites gave way to the tribes of Yahweh much more through conversion than by through death and destruction. "Canaanites" became "Israelites" through a radical conversion of faith and social practices. Thus, "Canaanite" and "Israelite" were ethnic identities less biological than socially constructed, a truth we are starting to learn about race and ethnicity all over again today.

The details of Gottwald's reading of tribal Israel and its liberating power in the historical context of ancient Canaan are beyond the scope of this chapter. But perhaps I have said enough to suggest parallels with that market day in Kendal in 1652. In proclaiming the day of the Lord, George Fox invoked divine power to breach the "walls," the structures of an unjust and unequal English society. And through that breach came men and women who hungered and thirsted for righteousness, just as the trumpets and shouts of the Israelites drew out restless elements from inside the walls of Jericho.

The day of the Lord is an event waiting to happen in every age, in every social context. In recent times we've seen similar developments, such as the Occupy Movement. Occupy grew out of the crisis of the financial meltdown. It drew together a wide range of groups that were either marginalized or that advocated causes of peace, justice and sustainability, causes that are still marginal in the present system. They gathered and circulated around fortresses of the present regime such as Wall Street, and they did a lot of shouting. Over time, Occupy seemed to disperse, ebb and fail. But we should look at it as part of a larger process, just as the story of Jericho is probably a symbolic representation of a much larger social and historical process.

The diverse and dispersed groups and causes that came together with Occupy, that gathered around the edges of the Paris climate summit, that continue coalescing in various Transition Towns, and so on, still lack a fully revolutionary faith like the Yahwism of ancient tribal Israel, or the early Quaker Lamb's War. Those movements were socially transcendent: they brought together very different kinds of people and concerns. That social transcendence was generated by a divine transcendent, the experience of a radically Other, who can unite us across our many kinds of human otherness.

I live in hope that something like that will emerge and unite us with greater power than we have seen so far. Friends are already involved in many ways and in many places in this process. But we can also draw upon biblical and early Quaker history to fire our political imaginations and inspire fresh insights and action.

# 7

## TO THE PEACEMAKERS:
## "LET THE WAVES BREAK OVER YOUR HEADS"

I HAVE TO admit, I'm not much of a "current events" Quaker. As a Friends pastor, I usually focus on the life of the meeting as a spiritual haven, an anchor for our lives of faithfulness, and a secure base from which we can make our social witness as we are led, as individuals or as a meeting. So my messages tend to generate out of my personal experience and my sense of the meeting. But with wave after wave of disturbing events in the world lately, even I find myself led to reflect with you on the state of our world and our country.

(Note: this message was given at Durham Friends Meeting in July 2016, between the two national political conventions. That summer had already seen videos of African American men killed by police followed by ambushes of police by snipers, the ongoing human catastrophe in Syria, terrorist attacks in Europe, thousands of refugees dying as they tried to get to Europe from Africa and the Middle East, and Europe itself looking more fragile.)

Of course, we may have different interpretations and points of emphasis on all this. But we can all see the troubles mounting. The sense of being overwhelmed by wave after wave reminded me of a letter George Fox wrote to the first Friends in 1652. It was the very beginning of the movement, and they were already getting in trouble. They weren't always looking for trouble, but their plain Quaker ways of speaking, dressing, and acting often offended people. And their criticisms of the state church were incendiary at a time when England was very unstable and the future uncertain.

So these first Friends found themselves in conflict, whether they were looking for it or not. Fox's letter begins by asserting this basic principle: "That which is set up by the sword, is held up by the sword; and that which is set up by spiritual weapons is held up by spiritual weapons, not by carnal weapons." In the aftermath of the English Civil War, the new Puritan establishment was using the sword to enforce its rule against Royalists to the right and against radical groups on the left. By contrast, Quakers believed that the beheading of Charles I in 1649 had opened a space for England's true sovereign, Christ Jesus, to rule the nation through the consciences of people freed from both monarchy and an enforced state church. Now that's a truly radical idea!

This new kingdom, the kingdom of heaven on earth, could be established and defended only by spiritual weapons. "Spiritual weapons"? That may seem like a contradiction of terms to many today, but it wasn't to early Friends. They understood that if you want to live a Spirit-led life, and help to build a more just society, you *will* face conflicts. You will face conflicts with yourself as you live into more Spirit-led patterns. And as you work with others for a more peaceful and just society, you'll face conflicts with those who want to keep things as they are. Peace, it turns out, is all about conflict. We don't have to go out and demonstrate or engage in civil disobedience to experience this conflict. We experience it daily in the decisions we make in how to live, in our interactions with neighbors and co-workers.

George continues; "The peace-maker has the kingdom and is in it; and has dominion over the peace-breaker, to calm him in the power of God." Fox could write these words with authority. He had already spent a year in prison. He had been beaten by angry mobs several times and threatened with deadly weapons. He had said things that got him in trouble. But he also possessed an inner calm and confidence in God that had unnerving effects on hostile people. This is not to say that he was confident that he wouldn't be hurt or even killed. It was a confidence that the power of God is present in every situation and can be change people's hearts, even—especially—in situations of conflict and even violence.

And we know this from our own experience, if we examine it. Each of us has seen how a kind word, a compassionate gesture, or simply acting with a calm confidence and an inner peace can alter situations. That's *authority* in the truest sense. It's being clear about what you need to do and say, and leaving others free to make their own decisions around that. It's stepping onto solid ground, into the kingdom, the realm of peace-making.

Now Fox gets to the line that came to my mind as I watched the news unfold: "And Friends, let the waves break over your heads. There is a new and living way coming out of the north, which makes the nations like waters." Early Friends, starting in northern England, were part of this new and living way. It was making waves all around them, and those waves were bound to come back at them. It was crucial not to panic, but to let the waves break over their heads; to be confident of God's power; to stay grounded in it.

Part of George Fox's genius consists in little counterintuitive phrases like that one. Like "stand still in the light." When you want to run away from the truth, or from trouble, "stand still in the light" and let it show you how things really are. "Contrary to your expectation," you will feel the warmth of God's love and the power to do the right thing, even if it's a big, scary thing for you. Or "sink down to the seed." When you feel as if you're sinking into despair and you're grasping at straws, "sink down to the seed." Stop flailing around and let yourself fall into hands of the living God, who is waiting to comfort, heal and renew you. That is where you learn to let God's power and wisdom act through you.

Somehow, "Let the waves break over your heads" feels like a word for our time. There is a growing turbulence in climate, economy, and society. All

---

of us are feeling it. Some Friends are wading further into it, witnessing and working for peace, justice, and sustainability. Others are standing still, waiting and watching. In either case, as we let the turbulence break over our heads, we keep our grounding as peacemakers and aren't panicked by the peace-breakers, those who want to respond to violence and injustice with more violence and injustice.

Not all of us are activists. But as we live into radical faithfulness with lives of integrity and truth-telling, enough conflict will find us. The world around us will do most of the moving. We only need to hold our ground in what we know, and the One we know. As we keep our footing in the peaceable kingdom, we will find the words to calm those who have lost their peace, and actions to comfort the afflicted. That's true authority, the power of God at work in us and through us.

# 8

## JAMES NAYLER AND THE LAMB'S WAR: "LED BY THE LAMB IN A WAY THEY KNOW NOT"

THE BOOK OF Revelation, the Apocalypse of John, is surely the most forbidding book of the New Testament. It was apparently challenging even in its own day. It was the last book to be admitted into the canon of the New Testament. Revelation was probably written more than sixty years after the death of Jesus, in the mid-90s of the first century. Already in the next century, it was seized upon by Montanists and other groups as a guide to predicting the end of the world. It has provided the grist for end-time predictions, strange cults, and Rapture maps ever since.

Revelation's disturbing flood of visions, symbols and violence repels most Friends today. But it is probably no worse than the daily torrent of horrific news and end-of-the-world action movies purveyed by the media today. In both cases, the key to withstanding the torrent is not to get swept up by the details, but to look for the larger patterns. What deep structures underlie what appears to be sheer chaos? A good diagnostician doesn't get too fixated on the symptoms but seeks to identify the disease itself, and how to help the body fight it.

The word "apocalypse" derives from the Greek root *apokalypsis*, which simply means a revelation, taking away the veil, seeing what's below the appearance of things. In the Book of Revelation, a first-century Christian prophet named John received a revelation of the true nature of the Roman Empire and the growing crisis early Christians faced, living in "the belly of the beast."

The violence depicted in Revelation is largely the violence of the Empire itself, revealed for what it is by the light that comes from the throne of heaven. Apocalyptic literature lays things bare not through modern investigative journalism but by using mythic language and symbol. That is often opaque and off-putting for us today, but that was "telling it like it is" to the ancient mind.

Another off-putting aspect of Revelation is John's sometimes vindictive tone toward the Romans. Modern scholars believe that John was a Palestinian Jewish Christian who had seen the Romans destroy Jerusalem and its temple, slaughter many thousands of his people, and drag 70,000 of them off into slavery elsewhere in the Empire.[26] That was in the year 70 of the Common Era, some forty years after the death of Jesus. The Roman defeat of the Jewish revolt was the worst single disaster in Jewish history until the Holocaust of the 20th century. Like many other Jewish Christians, John fled to Asia Minor (what is today modern Turkey), where he circulated as a prophet among early Christian congregations. He addresses seven of those churches in Revelation 2-3.

It is not hard, then, to imagine a post-traumatic element in John's voice. He had seen the end of his Jewish, temple-centered world, along with his own people's enormous suffering. He had survived one trauma and was trying to prepare the wider Christian movement for an impending one, the persecution of the early Church. He refers to Rome as "Babylon." The Babylonian Empire had destroyed Jerusalem and the first temple 600 years earlier.

But in Revelation, the "end of the world" is not a simple, linear, future-oriented question, the way we moderns tend to frame it. Although there is some future expectation in the book, in general, the structure of Revelation itself contains the End at all points. For John, to see Rome for what it really is exposes and ends its mystifying power, a power that keeps the world in wonder and captivity. Bedazzled by the power of Rome, people are blinded to the power of God, and alienated from the power to build a very different society. So Revelation offers an apocalypse that deconstructs, explodes the splendor of Rome, and unmasks Caesar as a false "savior" and a blasphemous "lord of the cosmos" (titles actually ascribed to him in that day).

It's an end that's already beginning. George Fox understood this when he read Revelation and looked at the society around him in the apocalyptic power of the light's revelation. He titled one of his books *The Great Mystery of the Great Whore Unfolded and Antichrist's Kingdom Revealed unto Destruction* (1659)—language straight out of the Book of Revelation. So what is in Fox's book? Wild visions or dire predictions? No, it is a large compendium of point-by-point answers to doctrinal attacks against Quakers by various Puritan clergy. Fox defends the Quaker message and counter-attacks the doctrines of his Puritan critics. It's very slow going, and nothing as exotic as the Book of Revelation.

But Fox viewed the state-enforced national church and its tithe-supported clergy as the Revelation's Beast and False Prophet in his time and place. He and early Friends saw the Church of England as the mystifying power that maintained an unjust and violent society. They called men and women to leave this Babylon and gather into groups to be taught by Christ who had "come to teach his people himself" and would lead them in creating a new, just, and peaceful society from the grassroots up. It was a second-coming message, in a sense. But Friends preached that Christ was not dropping out of the sky. Christ is present by a light that has always been in people's consciences everywhere—they just haven't paid attention to it. We touched upon some of that teaching from another angle in Chapter 4, with reference to Jacob in the Bible.

So the end of the world and the start of the kingdom of heaven on earth is always present and ready to happen. But Fox and early Friends saw how doctrinaire religion and social conformity kept people's minds alienated from it. They witnessed against many forms of social inequality, poverty, immorality, and violence in their society. But they viewed state-sponsored, coercive religion as the linchpin of the whole corrupt social structure.

Early Friends were not unique in their interest in the Book of Revelation. All kinds of radical groups read and speculated on it during this time of crisis in English society. But none of them turned it into a present experience and an unfolding social program as early Friends did. No group found themselves in the middle of the Book of Revelation as early Friends did. They viewed themselves as the radical vanguard that gathers around and follows the Lamb into nonviolent direct action, as portrayed in Revelation 14. Their name for their movement, The Lamb's War, was thus drawn from Revelation.

Crisis has been a recurring theme in these chapters. Apocalyptic language is the language of crisis. As noted in Chapter 1, the Greek word *krisis* means not only a critical moment, but a time of decision, of discernment, judgment. We find this stated most clearly in the Gospel of John (almost certainly a different John from the writer of the Apocalypse). In Chapter 3 of John's gospel, we hear Jesus say to Nicodemus, "this is the judgment [*krisis*], that the light has come into the world, and people loved the darkness rather than the light . . . so that their deeds may not be exposed. But those who do what is true come to the light, so that it may be clearly seen" (3:19-21). Judgment day is not someday in the future, but now and always. And it's a "do-it-yourself" judgment, as we either come to or flee from the light.

These verses are echoed in various ways in George Fox's writings, particularly his letters of spiritual counsel. Fox had a genius for teaching weary Seekers how to stand still in the light and let it show them how things really are, whether painful or reassuring. And if they would remain there, the same light would guide and empower them into a new life. Early Quaker epistles focus mainly on personal and group experience, much like the epistles of the

New Testament. But other early Quaker writings put that personal and group experience in the context of the social crisis of their time, like the Book of Revelation. They call people to become a community of transformed men and women working for the transformation of society. As William Penn summarized, "they were changed [people] themselves before they went about to change others."[27]

▲ ▲ ▲

James Nayler wrote the fullest description of the crisis that early Friends experienced and advanced upon English society. His tract *The Lamb's War* was written in 1657, while he was imprisoned in London. It was the year following his sensational show-trial before Parliament and the savage punishment he suffered for that they judged to be his "horrid blasphemy." What was Nayler's blasphemy, and what was so "horrid" about it? Parliament insisted that Nayler had dangerous messianic delusions. In October 1656, he and a small inner circle of followers performed a symbolic reenactment of Jesus entering Jerusalem, with Nayler in the starring role. During his interrogation, Nayler made it clear that he didn't consider himself to be Christ, but was enacting a sign of Christ. But Parliament chose to ignore his testimony because they wanted to stigmatize the Quaker movement's most charismatic leader, and to discredit the movement generally.[28]

But Nayler's real "horrid blasphemy," what really offended Parliament, was just what he had affirmed, and what early Friends were saying all along: Christ has come in the flesh of common people like James Nayler, a farmer from Hicksville, Yorkshire. That was a truly dangerous idea, with implications as much political as theological.

So as the storm around him settled, and as Nayler slowly recovered from Parliament's cruel treatment, he wrote a flat-out manifesto, titled *The Lamb's War*. This revolutionary ideology had appeared only in fragmentary forms in earlier Quaker writings. Let us take a few glimpses at Nayler's tract.

He makes it clear that the Lamb and those who follow the Lamb are engaged in a nonviolent struggle. But that struggle is sweeping in scope:

Their war is not against creatures, they wrestle not with flesh and blood which God hath made, but with spiritual wickedness, exalted in the hearts of men and women, where God alone should be . . . . Indeed their war is against the whole work and device of the god of this world, his laws, his customs, his fashions, his inventions, and all which are to add to or take from the work of God . . . . [The Lamb] comes to take the government to himself, that God may wholly rule in the heart of man, and man wholly live in the work of God.[29]

This is a breathtaking statement. Nayler describes a far-reaching cultural revolution. But it is nothing like Mao's cultural revolution in China during the 1960s, or various Islamic revolutions in more recent history. The key difference is that this cultural revolution spreads persuasively from below, rather than coercively from above.

Nayler makes this still clearer in the next paragraph:

And as they war not against men's persons, so their weapons are not carnal, nor hurtful to any of the creation; for the Lamb comes not to destroy men's lives, nor the work of God, and therefore at his appearance in his subjects, he puts spiritual weapons into their hearts and hands: their armor is the light, their sword is the Spirit of the Father and the Son; their shield is faith and patience, their paths are prepared with the gospel of peace and good will towards all the creation of God (see Ephesians 6:10-17).

Nayler goes on to describe the Lamb's realm:

His kingdom in this world, in which he chiefly delights to walk and make himself known, is in the hearts of such as have believed in him, and owned his call out of the world, whose hearts he hath purified, and whose bodies he hath washed in obedience . . . and in such he rejoices and takes delight . . . he leads them by the gentle movings of his Spirit out of all their own ways and wills . . . and guides them into the will of the Father . . . deeply he lets them know his covenant, and how far they may go and be safe . . . his presence is great joy to them of a willing mind.

So why hasn't the Lamb already won this spiritual conflict? Why isn't everyone with the Lamb? Nayler observes,

Many are ashamed at the Lamb's appearance, it is so low & weak & poor & contemptible, & many are afraid seeing so great a power against him; many be at work in their imaginations, to compass a kingdom to get power over sin, & peace of conscience, but few will deny all to be led by the Lamb in a way they know not, to bear his testimony & mark against the world, and to suffer for it with him.

By "compass a kingdom," Nayler means calculating, strategizing how to induce the kingdom of heaven. Other radicals of the time, such as the Fifth Monarchists, were given to such strategies, including violent attempts at insurrection. But the only way to participate in the Lamb's kingdom is to be led by the Lamb in a way one knows not. We heard Nayler testify to that path in Chapter 1, when he said that since he walked out the front gate of his home, he didn't know from one day to the next where he would be led. Certainly, he demonstrated just how far that path could go—within an inch of his life. Parliament chose not to execute him, because they realized it would only create greater problems. They had at least learned that much from the gospels. They had learned from the Romans' mistake, but not from the radical faithfulness of Jesus. That's what people do when they attempt to "compass a kingdom" instead of live faithfully.

We today need to consider where the mystifying power of our own violent and unjust society resides. I've made a try at that in my recent book, *The Anti-War*.[30] It's a call to Friends to become more than "anti-war," as an adjective, a position; to become the anti-war, a substantive way of being in the world, an inversion of today's military-industrial complex—a beast as horrific as anything in the Book of Revelation.

Answering the call to radical faithfulness covers the full gamut of our faith and practice. It's our personal practices of spiritual formation, seeking at that deeper level that Sarah Jones, Sarah Blackborow and Frances Howgill witnessed. It's mentoring others into that deeper search as they did. It can mean making your home a hospitality center and meeting place for faithful witnesses, as Margaret Fell did. It can mean exposing deceit in the marketplace, as George Fox did that day at Kendal. It can also mean putting yourself on the line as a sign of the Lamb, as James Nayler did.

As we read the Bible, and helpful books about the Bible, with the fresh eyes of radical faithfulness, it will tell us new things, and sound surprisingly contemporary. As Mary Morrison commented some years ago, discussing her Gospels course at Pendle Hill, the Bible is like the oracle at Delphi in ancient Greece: the answers we receive from the Bible will depend on the questions we bring to it.[31]

# 9

## JOHN CAMM'S BRILLIANT FAILURE

THE QUAKER WAY is one of experimentation. When Fox heard the voice telling him, "There is one, even Christ Jesus, that can speak to thy condition," he adds, "this I knew experimentally."[32] He meant that he knew it by personal experience. But this knowledge came by way of his lonely experiment in seeking: turning his back on the standard religious answers—and the alternative ones, too—to find a deeper truth. But in both science and faith, failure is an important part of experimentation. And we learn from failure as much as we do from success: think of Thomas Edison and the 99 ways he discovered *not* to make a light bulb. This story from the early ministry of John Camm is a story of apparent failure.

John Camm was a farmer in northern England in the 1650s. John and his wife Mabel (mentioned in Chapter 1) were part of a group of a thousand Seekers, church dropouts, who heard George Fox preach on a hilltop called Firbank Fell in June 1652. Both John and Mabel Camm were reached by Fox's message that day. They soon joined the traveling Quaker prophets who spread across the countryside with the Quaker message.

Two years later, in 1654, John felt God calling him to spread the Quaker message to Oxford. This was very hostile territory. Oxford University was a bastion of the Church of England. Young men studied there to become priests in this state-sponsored church. Now, John Camm was not an educated man: in his correspondence, his grammar and spelling are all over the place. And there he was, a rustic farmer from the North, trying to convert these young university men of privilege and with career expectations in the church.

Even worse, he was trying to get them to leave the Church of England and join these notorious, ragtag Quakers, who were out to disestablish the very church they were preparing to serve. The response was not just uninterested; it was hostile. Two young Quaker women, Mary Fisher and Elizabeth Williams, tried the same thing in Cambridge. They were physically abused by the students, arrested by the authorities, and flogged through the streets of Cambridge.

Camm attempted a more low-profile approach. But after some weeks of effort, all he had to show for his time in Oxford was one solid convert: not a student, but a local tradesman named Thomas Loe. Pretty much a failure by standard measures. Fortunately, Camm went on to great success later that year preaching with John Audland in Bristol. For his part, Loe soon began to travel and preach on his own. And one day in 1656, he had an encounter with a 12-year-old upper-class boy named William Penn. William was an earnest young Puritan, and he was powerfully affected by Loe's message. But he wasn't yet ready to forsake the privilege and promise of his upper-class circumstances. And his father, no less than the Lord Admiral of the British Navy, was definitely not having a Quaker in the family. But a seed was planted. And eleven years later in 1667, William Penn, now aged 23, ran into Thomas Loe again. This time, he knew he had to become a Quaker, even though it would alienate his family and make him a pariah among his wealthy Puritan friends.

Now, you may have never heard of John Camm or Thomas Loe before. But you know of William Penn. You don't have to be a Quaker to know about Penn, the Quaker founder of Pennsylvania. When he received the royal charter in 1680 for a new colony in America, he called it a "Holy Experiment." It was an experiment to "try what love can do," as he put it. Penn's experiment in love included peaceful and friendly relations with the native peoples, making treaties with them and buying land from them. He advertised his colony across Europe as a haven for persecuted peoples. Pennsylvania became the most tolerant and peaceful colony in America. It was a world's fair of funny little sects and social outcasts from Europe. Penn's experiment was a major influence in shaping religious freedom and democratic government in the formative stages of our country.

By the time Pennsylvania was starting in the New World, the more revolutionary Quaker experiment, the Lamb's War, had been defeated in England by governmental persecution and by an English population that preferred to return the verities of a more hierarchical, less experimental life. The first generation of Friends were not wrong about the return of Christ by his light in the human conscience, but not enough people were ready to turn in that direction. Friends were not wrong about "the day of the Lord," and the coming of the kingdom of heaven on earth, but the restored kingdom of Charles II successfully fended it off, and most people were relieved. God respects human freedom. But God also afforded William Penn an astonishing opportunity to try a less revolutionary but bold experiment in a new land.

We can never predict the catalyzing effects of a faithful word or a loving action. We're always operating in the dark, really. We have our good intentions and leadings. But the actual outcomes may be very different from anything we expected. John Camm's time in Oxford seemed like a failure. But the one Quaker he made in Oxford changed the life of William Penn, and William Penn made a major difference in English and American history.

As people of faith, we grope our way, trying to follow a God whose purposes work in patterns that vastly outdistance what we can see and understand. As the prophet Isaiah put it, we're following a God whose thoughts are not our thoughts, whose ways are not our ways (Isa. 55:8-9). In fact, Isaiah's life is an excellent example. He was called one day to be a messenger of the

Lord to his people Israel. And after some hesitation, Isaiah answered, "Here I am, send me." And then God said, "Great, but nobody's going to get it. They'll listen but not really hear; they'll look but not see what you're talking about." So Isaiah answered, "Oh, and for how long, O Lord?" And the Lord said, "Quite a while" (see Isa. 6).

Isaiah's prophetic career was a failure. He tried to reform his people, but they didn't get it. 700 years later, Jesus often quoted from Isaiah during his own ministry. But not many understood Jesus either. When they didn't even fathom his little parables, he quoted from Isaiah 6 (see Mark 4:11-12). Only after he was gone did people begin to understand, begin to believe, begin to share in his faith. And the prophecies of Isaiah in particular helped them understand who Jesus really was. The New Testament gospels are peppered with quotations from Isaiah.

This may sound familiar to readers who are parents. You keep trying to get some basic points across, but they don't seem to register with your sons and daughters until some years later. I recall Mark Twain's remark that when he was 16 he couldn't believe how stupid his father was. But by 18, after a couple years on his own, he was amazed at how wise his father had become.

All we can do is keep our intentions pure. All we can do is keep speaking the truth in love the best we can. Keep following those little nudges we get to speak kindly, to act generously. It helps to maintain an active prayer life. It sharpens our insight into people and situations. Our hearts will grow more tender to the suffering of others. And we will become more attuned to those little nudges from God about how to respond. In the final analysis, all we can do is keep the experiment of faith alive: offer it up and let God work with our efforts in some larger pattern we can't see. It keeps us humble, but it also keeps us hopeful.

# 10

## GEORGE FOX'S DYING WORDS: "I'M GLAD I WAS HERE"

I WANT TO offer one more reflection on radical faithfulness, taking another lesson from the rich treasury of early Quaker history. I have learned a lot from listening to the voices of early Friends and trying to understand what their words meant in the context of their times. They have enriched my own faith, as I have tried to "feel the place where the words come from," to use that wonderful phrase from John Woolman's *Journal.*[33]

In this chapter I return again to George Fox. Someone once teased me, saying that I'm a George Fox channeler. When I first started reading Fox's *Journal* in 1976, I have to admit that I was a bit put off. Like the apostle Paul's, Fox's personality is an acquired taste for many. Perhaps someone like Paul or Fox, who keeps getting attacked verbally and physically for his witness, but keeps bouncing back, isn't going to be Mr. Lovable. But I've learned a lot from both of them. Isaac Penington was in awe of Fox, writing that he saw into things more deeply than others. William Penn also admired Fox greatly. He called Fox "no man's copy," an original. His genius derived from his ability to keep returning to the source and keep drawing from it. Penn writes, "The most awful, living, reverent frame I ever felt or beheld was his in prayer . . . he knew and lived nearer to the Lord than other men."[34] And of course, Margaret Fell even married him.

I want to share with you in this chapter some of Fox's dying words. Though he had a robust constitution, his time in England's lousy, septic jails over the years took a toll on his health. He died in January 1691, in the 67th year of his life. He collapsed after preaching at a meeting of Friends in London and died a few days later. The small circle of friends at his bedside recorded some of his dying words. Among them were the words, "All is well. . . . The Seed reigns over all unruly spirits."

As you know, Fox and other early Friends used the word seed for the divine life that abides within each of us. It rises and grows to new life if we turn to it and nurture it through prayer and meditation, through lives of love and service. That seed is the eternal in us. Eternity is not something that starts when we run out of time. Eternity is the *hidden dimension* of time. As we learn to live from that eternal source within ourselves, we are already becoming part of heaven in this life.

When the Quaker Mary Dyer was being led to the gallows on Boston Common in 1659, someone in the crowd sought to console her, saying she would be in paradise soon. Mary Dyer replied that she had been in paradise for a couple of weeks now. She had faithfully lived out her testimony to the world, in the face of savage Puritan hostility. Now she had gathered herself into the eternal seed and could face death with peace of mind.

Maybe "peace of mind" is a relative term when we face death. Even if you're well grounded in eternity, facing the end of this life is probably terrifying to all of us. I think that's what Fox meant by the seed reigning over all "unruly spirits." The human fear of death wanted to take over his mind. But from a deeper place, the seed reigned over—reined in—those very human fears.

Fox also taught that although the divine seed is sown in each person, ultimately, there is just one seed. We are all one in that seed. Fox bases his teaching on Paul's point in Galatians 3:16 that the promise of God is to the one seed, Christ. Fox's teaching comes through with particular clarity in a letter he wrote to Friends when Edward Burrough died. Burrough was one of the great early Quaker leaders and had brought many in London to the Quaker movement. When he died in prison in 1663, still in his twenties, it rocked the movement. Fox wrote to comfort and reassure Friends: "Be still and wait in your own conditions, and settled in the Seed of God that doth not change, that in that [Seed] ye may feel dear Edward Burrough among you in the Seed, in which and by which he begat you to God, with whom he is: and that in the Seed ye may all see and feel him, and in [the Seed] is unity in the life with him. And so enjoy him in the life that doth not change, but which is invisible."[35]

In the eternal seed we can feel those who have passed on before us. In that seed we feel unity with all others in this life. In the seed we feel a particular unity with those whose lives embody and promote peace, justice, and unity with the rest of God's creation. It all joins together in the seed. And as we learn to sink down to that seed within, learn to rest there, and learn to draw from its strength and guidance, we are living eternity now.

But my favorite of the last words of George Fox are these: "I'm glad I was here. Now I am clear, I am fully clear."[36] When Fox uses the word "clear," he usually means being clear about what he needs to do, and then having done that, clear of that responsibility. It's about being a good servant of the Lord. Fox suffered a lot—from persecution by hostile opponents, and sometimes from wrangling with other Friends. Most of all, he carried the burden of starting a revolutionary religious movement, and suffering the disappointment of its failure to transform English society. He suffered serious bouts of depression at various times in his life. But at the end of all that, he could say, "I'm glad I was here. Now I am clear, I am fully clear."

"I'm glad I was here." It's an intriguing affirmation at the end of life. It implies a lot. The existential philosopher Martin Heidegger called existence *Dasein*, literally, "being there," or "there-being." To exist is to be somewhere. We don't exist except in particular times and places. When we die, we no longer exist, any more than God exists. (Another existentialist philosopher, Soren Kierkegaard, wrote, "God does not exist; God is eternal.") When we die, we move fully into eternity, which is in God, which is neither here nor there. Again, that's the dimension hidden in our existence all along—what Fox called the seed.

In this life, sometimes God feels present, here with us; at other times, God feels absent. But perhaps God is neither present nor absent. God abides and walks with us at the interface between eternity and time. That's our life in the seed.

# PART II

QUAKER FAITH AND PRACTICE:
A COVENANTAL LIFE

# 11

## COVENANT IN QUAKER SPIRITUAL FORMATION

IN PART I of this collection, we focused on the early Quaker experience of calling and faithfulness. These concepts generate from the biblical tradition of covenant. Covenant is not a word we hear much in our meetings today, but covenant is part of our experience, whether it's named or not. Think of the most familiar form of covenant in relationship—marriage, or any long-term, committed relationship. There are ways we "call" one another into that relationship, and keep calling one another back into that relationship as our life circumstances keep changing—indeed, as we keep changing. There's a "faithfulness" that we embody toward one another as we continue answering one another's call. We live faithfully to the love we have for one another. We live into a kind of shared *integrity*, a oneness, a wholeness that is more than the sum of our two persons. Integrity is speaking and living the truth as best as we can.

Faithfulness to the truth gets back to the Old English word for truth: *troth*. "I pledge my troth" is an old expression in some wedding vows. It expresses that sense of truth as integrity, faithfulness. Truth is not just *propositional*, a matter of true or false statements. Truth is *participational*: we live it or we don't.

But inevitably along the way, we fail. We make mistakes, we're insensitive to one another, we demand too much, we stray or fall prey to one of the many ways that covenant relationship gets tested over time. So another key aspect of covenant relationship is forgiveness, the willingness to let past mistakes go and start over with one another. Indeed, forgiveness is one of the ways we call each other back, invite each other to start over.

Covenant is a concept that addresses not only religious faith and interpersonal relationships. It has inspired modern political thought as well. Federal and confederal forms of government generated out of Reformation and early Quaker political application of covenantal theology from the Bible (the Latin for covenant is *foedus*, the root of our word "federal"). I give some attention to the biblical roots and larger meanings of covenant in *The Covenant Crucified: Quakers and the Rise of Capitalism*.[37] Covenant is a powerful and remarkably simple framework for grappling with the complexity and messiness of life, relationship, and political realities.

Let us begin by briefly reviewing some basic words and concepts from the Bible. The whole history narrated by the Hebrew and Christian Scriptures can be seen as a series of covenants that God initiates with humans, trying to restore peace and balance among humans, and to the way humans live upon the earth. The original, unconditional blessing of man and woman as stewards of the creation (Gen. 1:27-30) is implicitly a covenant. But as violence and injustice spread among humans, God starts over with a more explicit approach in calling Abraham and Sarah, promising unconditionally to make them a great nation. God remains faithful to that promise. Abraham and Sarah are faithful as well, with some stumbles here and there. The covenant with Israel through Moses finds God promising more conditionally. There's a long list of conditions—laws—that Israel must follow as covenant becomes a fully fledged social order. The full body of laws comprises a constitution of sorts.

The new covenant given through Jesus in the Christian Scriptures expands the covenant toward all humanity, but this time as a network of communities rather than a sovereign territory. It is unconditional in character: God's love has been communicated to all humanity through the life, teachings, and death of Jesus. All are called, invited to live into that love in ever-expanding circles. But in the concreteness of actual faith community, some actions are more faithful than others. As Paul writes, "All things are lawful, but not all things are beneficial" (1 Cor. 10:23).

To be sure, much more could be said about the covenants in the Bible, the various ways humans failed in each, and the various ways God starts over with us. And, to be sure, there are some ugly, bloody parts of that saga. The Bible is the story of oppression and violence as well as liberation and peacemaking. Living as part of a faith tradition means that we need to remember both. That is part of living into the covenant. Covenant relationship always has a history—but it also has a future.

What is the quality of covenant relationship? Old Testament scholar Gerhard von Rad[38] identified *shalom* as the Hebrew word most often used to define covenant relationship. "Peace" is a very inadequate translation of *shalom*, which implies a wholeness of relationship, a communion, a state of equity, a harmonious equilibrium, a balancing of claims and needs among parties. The Hebrew word for covenant is *berith*, whose verb-form means "to bind together" (much as "religion" means "rebinding"). But paradoxically, the verb often used in Hebrew to describe making a covenant is *karath*, which means "to cut." One *cuts a covenant* (perhaps our idiom to "cut a deal" echoes that usage).

Binding and cutting imply each other. As we live faithfully into relationship with another, as our lives are increasingly bound together, we find that we can no longer do everything we earlier felt free to do. We have to let some things go. We find ourselves willing to make some cuts here and there for the sake of the more fulfilling *shalom* we are finding together.

One more Hebrew word to mention in relation to covenant is *adoth*, which translates "testimony," or "witness," or sometimes "covenant." "Testament" is of course a cognate of "testimony." We think of the Old and New Testaments as the collections of Hebrew and Greek writings. But really the writings are historic witness to the testaments, the covenants themselves. We Quakers sometimes have a similar confusion. When someone mentions Quaker "faith and practice," we often assume that they're referring to our book of discipline. But Quaker faith and practice is the thing itself, a covenantal life. The book describes it.

In the Christian Scriptures, the word most used for covenant is the Greek *diakethe*. In ancient Greek usage, *diatheke* usually meant a last will, a "dying testament." That of course describes the last supper of Jesus with his disciples before his death, as described in the New Testament gospels, where he sealed his covenant with them. The New Testament word for witness or testimony is the Greek *martyria*, the root of our word "martyr." In the New Testament, *martyria* implies words or actions that communicate the gospel, the good news of Jesus—which of course did sometimes lead to martyrdom.

Of course, covenant is a term in modern legal language as well. A covenant is a binding obligation, often perpetual, undertaken voluntarily by parties and often premised on some shared sense of divine will or ethical principle, such as universal human rights. By contrast, contracts tend to be limited in term and narrowly defined according to the interests of the two or more parties that agree. Forgiveness is usually not part of the deal. Legal retaliation is more likely the outcome of unfaithfulness to a contract.

This very brief introduction to some key terms and concepts of covenant in the Bible should be useful as we now explore the Quaker approach to covenant.

⋏ ⋏ ⋏

Early Friends used the language of covenant to speak of their experience of the light or seed within. This was partly because covenant was an important concept in the Puritan theology of their social environment. Puritans spoke of the covenant of grace, mediated by the atoning death of Jesus. But this grace was not intended for everyone—only for those whom God had chosen, elected before the beginning of time. This of course is the Calvinist doctrine of predestination. Some souls are destined for salvation, others for damnation (also known as reprobation).

But how could you know which one was your destiny? Puritan ministers assured their congregants that if they went to church regularly, prayed often, worked hard, and were a good citizen and family member, these were signs of God's grace at work. You're in the covenant! That counsel worked for many people, and motivated a great deal of religious devotion, hard work, and good citizenship. But more introspective, morally scrupulous souls, the hyper-Puritans who often became the first Friends, were driven to distraction by this counsel. How could they tell they weren't just fooling themselves? How could they *know* God, and not just *surmise* a relationship with the divine?

**Isaac Penington** was one such hyper-Puritan in his youth. He writes,

My heart from my childhood was pointed towards the Lord, whom I feared and longed after from my tender years . . . . And indeed I did sensibly receive of his love, of his mercy, and of his grace . . . . But I was exceedingly entangled about election and reprobation (having drunk in that doctrine . . . held forth by the strictest of those that were termed Puritans . . . [I feared that] notwithstanding all my desires and seekings after the Lord, he might in his decree have passed me by; and I felt it would be bitter to me to bear his wrath, and to be separated from his love for evermore.

After a period of ministry with a independent congregation in London, Penington was swept up briefly in the Ranter rebellion of 1649-50 (see Chapter 4). He despaired of his Puritan faith and lapsed briefly into a kind of moral nihilism, what he called a "fool's paradise." After a year in real upheaval and torment, he settled into six years of depression and withdrawal, until he started talking to Quakers around London in 1656. He was an intellectual who could easily out-debate these rustics from the North every time they met. But he also realized that they had a kind of joy and spiritual power he lacked. Finally, in 1658, after he and his wife Mary began worshipping with Friends, something shifted. He writes,

> The Lord opened my spirit, the Lord gave me the certain and sensible feeling of the pure seed, which had been with me from the beginning . . . and gave me such an inward demonstration and feeling of the seed of life, that I cried out in my spirit: *This is he, this is he; there is not another, there never was another. He was always near me, though I knew him not . . . oh that I might now be joined to him, and he alone might live in me.* . . . The light of life, which God hath hid in the heart, is the covenant; and from this covenant God doth not give knowledge to satisfy the vast, aspiring, comprehending wisdom of man; but living knowledge to feed that which is quickened by him; which knowledge is given in the obedience, and is very sweet and precious to the state of him that knows how to feed upon it.[39]

Early Friends spoke of the covenant of light, rather than the Puritan covenant of grace. The light is God's faithful, abiding presence in every human heart, or conscience. God waits for us there, calling with a voice we don't notice. This is not predestination: the light is there in everyone, not just a few. But as we hear Penington say, it's not there to satisfy our inquiring minds or overbearing wills. It is knowledge given in obedience. That is, we gain more light as we follow its motions faithfully. And as God has been waiting upon us all this time, we have to learn how to wait for the light's teaching, to "wait upon the Lord," as early Friends would say.

**Sarah Jones** is a mysterious figure who may or may not have become a Quaker, as we noted in Chapter 4. In 1650, she wrote to forlorn Seekers, "Stand still and see the salvation of God, which is in the light of his Covenant, which will stretch forth the hand of his power, as he did to Peter when he feared the proud waves would have prevailed over him. . . . Therefore come down, come down to the Word of his patience, which is nigh in your hearts."[40] Again, we hear the language of surrender to a covenant that is always already with us.

**Francis Howgill**, whom we met briefly in Chapter 4, had been a leading preacher among the northern Seekers before his Quaker convincement. He witnesses,

> He who is the Light is the Covenant, and he who is the Covenant is the Light, for they are one in him. And this covenant of peace is tendered to you who are far off . . . and so in the covenant of life abide, and you will see he is near you. . . . This gift is free, and offered freely to all who will receive it; and yet you cannot receive the gift in your own wills, but through the denial of your own will.[41]

So, just as the light is given to all and not just a predestined few, it is also not a matter of our own free will to accept it or not. Entering the light/covenant requires a surrender to the divine life within ("Wait in the light," as Fox writes; or "Sink down to the seed," as Penington writes). We come into the covenant as we abide faithfully in the light as it abides faithfully in us. There we may receive fresh insights and guidance in the particulars of our own lives.

⨠ ⨠ ⨠

The language of covenant is particularly strong among early Friends. It can still be heard throughout most of our history, though it fades in Quaker writings of the past century. Still, the logic of covenantal calling and faithfulness can be heard among some of our best spiritual guides. Thomas Kelly's *Testament of Devotion* is all about training our hearts and minds to maintain a state of inward prayer, a communion with the divine that refocuses and redirects our lives. In the opening essay, "The Light Within," he writes,

Deep within us all there is an amazing inner sanctuary of the soul, a holy place, a Divine Center, a speaking Voice, to which we may continuously return. Eternity is at our hearts, pressing upon our time-torn lives, warming us with intimations of an astounding destiny, calling us home to Itself. Yielding to these persuasions, gladly committing ourselves in body and soul, utterly and completely, to the Light Within, is the beginning of true life.

Let us explore together the secret of a deeper devotion, a more subterranean sanctuary of the soul, where the Light Within never fades, but burns, a perpetual Flame . . . if we are deadly in earnest in our dedication to the Light, and are willing to pass out of first stages into mature religious living . . . . What is here urged are internal practices and habits of the mind. What is here urged are secret habits of unceasing orientation of the deeps of our being about the Inward Light.[42]

In the inward life, as in our committed relationships and our religious community, faithfulness is 90% about showing up. At the end of a short but remarkable life, Thomas Kelly left us this testament – his testimony to the joy and sustaining strength he found in keeping the heart close to God.

In more recent years, influenced by a technological society all around us, we Friends tend to focus on the techniques of a Spirit-led life, the processes of making Spirit-led decisions together. Rex Ambler's *Experiment with Light* speaks to our condition today. He drew upon George Fox's letters of spiritual counsel to create a guided meditation that has been useful to many of us today. And there too, in Step 5, we can hear the echoes of covenantal faithfulness. Ambler writes,

When the answer comes, welcome it. It may be painful, or difficult to believe with your normal conscious mind, but if it is the truth you will recognize it immediately and realise that it is something that you need to know. Trust the light. Say yes to it. Submit to it. It will then begin to heal you. It will show you new possibilities for your life. It will show you the way through. So however bad the news seems to be at first, accept it and let its truth pervade your whole being.[43]

Whatever changes in our language and emphasis, Quaker spiritual formation always comes down to trust in a covenant partner, however understood, a Thou who calls forth a faithful "yes" from the core of our being.

I hope these specimen quotes from friends over the centuries begin to make sense of covenant as the heart of our Quaker experience. But more importantly, I hope the evocative language of these Quaker writers speaks to your own experience of being called and responding faithfully.

# 12

## COVENANT IN QUAKER WORSHIP, MINISTRY, AND DECISION-MAKING

GOD ABIDES FAITHFULLY with us, waiting for us to respond, to come into relationship, communion, and to become covenant partners in renewal of creation, in the work for a more peaceful, just, and sustainable world. We turn now to the ways Quaker worship and vocal ministry answer the call to radical faithfulness. More than 50 years ago now, Lewis Benson was the first to notice that George Fox understood Christ primarily as a prophet, not only in the lifetime of Jesus of Nazareth, but as the light that speaks a living word within us, and sometimes through us in vocal ministry. Fox insisted that early Friends were in the same spirit and power as the prophets and apostles of the Hebrew and Christian Scriptures. Quaker faith and practice is a prophetic spirituality. It's also accurate to call it a group mysticism, but prophetic is a more fitting term. Like mysticism, it is grounded in firsthand experience. But that experience leads us to speak and act in the world, not simply to enjoy a sense of oneness with God and with everything.

The prophets, from Moses onward, are the men and women who developed the covenantal understanding of God and community that we find in the Hebrew Bible. And the prophets, from Elijah through Amos, Jeremiah, Isaiah, and on down to today, keep calling their people back into a more faithful relationship with the Lord, who wills a peaceful and equitable society—a covenantal society.

The practice of the prophets is to wait upon the Lord to be called and given a word to speak or an action to carry out. This practice is found not only among the Hebrew prophets but among the early Christian apostles and congregations. Paul describes such a practice in 1 Corinthians 14. The truth of the prophetic word is not just a matter of accuracy to present and future facts. That is a *propositional* sense of truth. Prophetic truth is more fundamentally *participational*. It arises from faithful relationship with the divine and with others. This is truth as *troth*, that archaic English word we noted earlier. *Truth is being true*, living in faithful relationship.

But in the centuries after the New Testament canon was formed, it became common for Christians to think of the word of God as the written word of Scripture. That tendency grew with the invention of the printing press and the availability of printed Bibles. The Puritans were very focused on the word as Scripture. But by the time Quakers came along, the Puritans had split into many different interpretations of Scripture, with different creeds based on Scripture and different churches, each claiming to be based chapter-and-verse upon the New Testament example. Scripture was losing its standing as an objective source of truth. Quakers returned to the prophetic and apostolic sense of the living word, the word that gave rise to Scripture, but which needs to be freshly revealed in every generation, to every person. We can know the truth of Scripture only as we live faithfully, true to the Spirit that inspired it.

That was a radical approach in a number of ways. For one thing, it overturned the vested authority of university-trained clergy in the English state-church. In Chapter 1, we heard the story of Ann Audland and her confrontation with the parish priest in the town of Banbury. She told him that he was at odds with the doctrine of Christ. By doctrine, she meant not creeds about Christ, but the practice of speaking according to what one receives from the light of Christ. She told him that without the light's leading, he could say "the Lord liveth" and he would be speaking "falsely."[44] That was apparently the final provocation that put her in prison for blasphemy. Her point was that you can say something that may be propositionally true enough; but if you're not speaking not from personal revelation, it is not faithfully true. You're not participating in the truth. You're speaking false*ly*. This is key to understanding the Quaker approach to worship and ministry.

The Seekers who became the first Friends were women and men, mostly young, who yearned painfully to be part of a church they could believe in. With the array of churches, creeds, liturgies, and sacramental rites cropping up left and right, they ached to worship God in a form they could believe "was undoubtedly his own," as Mary Penington put it.[45] Quaker silent waiting upon the Lord was the breakthrough that thousands embraced all across England, within a very short time. But the itinerant prophets who convinced these Seekers had to spend time helping them know how to wait upon the Lord, how to stand still in the light, to find that place of stillness within, as we saw in Chapters 3 and 4. It didn't come easily for them any more than it does for us. But since they had been searching for so long and so desperately, when these Seeker groups finally found it, it was a powerful, cathartic experience.

One of the most famous descriptions of that breakthrough comes from Francis Howgill, whose witness to the covenant in personal experience we heard in the preceding chapter. He testifies to the powerful, pentecostal experience of the Westmorland Seekers in the summer of 1652:

> The Lord of Heaven and Earth we found to be near at hand; and as we waited upon him in pure Silence, our Minds out of all things, his Dreadful Power . . . appeared in our Assemblies, when there was no Language, Tongue nor Speech from any Creature, and the Kingdom of Heaven did gather us, and did catch us all, as in a Net . . . that we came to know a place to stand in, and what to wait in, and the Lord appeared daily to us, to our Astonishment, Amazement, and great Admiration, insomuch that we often said one to another, with great

joy of Heart, "What, is the Kingdom of God come to be with men?"
. . . And from that Day forward our Hearts were knit unto the Lord,
and one unto another, in truth and fervent Love, not by any External
Covenant . . . but we entered into the Covenant of Life with God.[46]

Again we hear the language of covenant. These men and women found themselves being "knit" into God and into one another. This was not just a novel
experience but a new life, one that would grow into many different kinds of
radical faithfulness.

As we noted in the preceding chapter, the language of covenant fades
from Quaker writings, especially over the last century. But we can still detect
an abiding covenantal logic and its major themes. Thomas Kelly's beautiful
essay, "The Gathered Meeting," gives sublime expression to the Quaker meeting for worship at its best:

In the practice of group worship on the basis of silence come spe-
cial times when the electric hush and solemnity and depth of power
steals over the worshipers. A blanket of divine covering comes over
the room, a stillness that can be felt is over all, and the worshipers are
gathered into a unity and synthesis of life which is amazing indeed.

Vocal prayer, poured out from a humble heart, frequently shifts a
meeting from a heady level of discussion to the deeps of worship. Such
prayers serve as an unintended rebuke to our shallowness and drive us
deeper into worship, and commitment. They open the gates of devotion, adoration, submission, confession. They help to unite the group
at the level at which real unity is sought. For unity in the springs of
life's motivations is far more significant than unity in phrases or outward manners.[47]

I hope all of us have felt such a gathered, or covered, meeting at least occa-
sionally in our lives as Friends. There's nothing quite like it. And when Kelly

speaks of vocal ministry, he emphasizes that prayer is often what brings the group to that deeper place. Vocal prayer is seldom heard in many meetings today. But it still can create that shift in a group. Prayer makes the covenant relationship more explicit. It reminds me of a quote from Martin Buber, the great Jewish religious philosopher. Before World War I, someone asked him if he believed in God. He answered, "If to believe in God means to be able to speak about Him in the third person, I do not believe in God. . . . But if to believe in God means to say 'Thou' to Him, then I do."[48] Our faith-convictions are bound to grow faint when our faithful, covenantal conversation with God lapses.

Kelly goes on to write of the more common experience of the ungathered—perhaps even scattered—meeting. He observes,

> Like the individual soul, the group must learn to endure spiritual weather without dismay. Some hours of worship are full of glow and life, but others lack the quality. The disciplined soul, and the disciplined group, have learned to cling to the reality of God's presence, whether the feeling of presence is great or faint. If only the group has been knit about the very springs of motivation, the fountain of the will, then real worship has taken place. If the wind of the Spirit, blowing whither He wills, warms the group into an inexpressible sense of unity, then the worshipers are profoundly grateful. If no blanket of divine covering is warmly felt, and *if wills have been offered together in the silent work of worship*, the worshipers may go home content and nourished, and say, "It was a good meeting." In the venture of group worship, souls must learn to accept spiritual "weather" and go deeper, in will, to Him who makes all things beautiful in their time.[49]

Both here and in the previous quotation, Kelly speaks of "the springs of motivation" as the key: not spiritual technique, the form of words spoken, nor even whether the group experiences gathering or not. That "knitting" of the group at the springs of motivation is the heart of covenant faithfulness. It's about "showing up" at the deepest level, where our "wills [are] offered together."

A more recent witness to the heart of Quaker worship and ministry was Bill Taber, the Ohio Conservative Friend who taught for many years at Pendle Hill. His pamphlet *Four Doors to Meeting for Worship* is a favorite of many Friends today. Taber was a recorded minister in Ohio Yearly Meeting. He writes of his growth in understanding what his ministry meant. He witnesses that over time,

> I came to *know* what I had merely *believed* before – that my ministry belonged to the meeting, not to me. I discovered that while the effectiveness of my ministry did depend somewhat on my faithfulness, it depended far more than I had realized on the invisible, hidden faithfulness of people who seldom if ever spoke in meeting.[50]

Again, the living truth of our worship and ministry is our *troth*, our faithful abiding with one another in the divine presence. It recalls to my mind the traditional response after meeting to a Friend who has spoken *truly* in ministry: "Thee was faithful."

▲ ▲ ▲

The Quaker meeting for business is a further covenantal call to radical faithfulness. One of my favorite statements on our business process comes from early Quaker Edward Burrough. He wrote this to Friends in London, many of whom he had himself convinced, in 1662. That was less than a year before he would die in Newgate prison for his radical faithfulness. Burrough counsels,

> Being orderly come together . . . proceed in the wisdom of God, not in the way of the world, as a worldly assembly of men, by hot contests, by seeking to out-speak and over-reach one another . . . as if it were controversy between party and party . . . or two sides violently

striving for dominion, not deciding affairs by the greater vote. But in the wisdom, love and fellowship of God, in gravity, patience, meekness, and unity and concord, submitting one to another in lowliness of heart, and in the holy Spirit of truth and righteousness . . . hearing, and determining every matter . . . in love, coolness, gentleness and dear unity; I say as one . . . party, all for the truth of Christ, and for the carrying on of the work of the Lord, and assisting one another.[51]

Notice how many qualitative words Burrough uses: patience, gravity, gentleness, coolness. The "dear unity" we strive for is a *quality* we sense among us. Voting simply *quantifies, measures* the degree of relative agreement and disagreement. It's more a contract, a deal, than a covenant. Decisions made in unity are much like working things through in a marriage, that form of covenant we know with or without a religious framework.

Bill Taber's posthumous Pendle Hill Pamphlet, *The Mind of Christ*, was edited by Michael Birkel from manuscripts and notes Taber had left. It offers a valuable companion piece to his *Four Doors to Meeting for Worship*, as it moves from worship to the business meeting among Friends. Like Edward Burrough, Taber evokes the *quality* of Quaker group discernment, rather than reducing it to process and technique. He writes,

When opinions differ widely and the need for spiritual discernment becomes crucial, the best of Quaker business techniques alone will not suffice; then we are driven . . . to seek that spiritual covering which alone can . . . sustain harmony while waiting for the right leading. Thus, God's work among us becomes more real, and faith is both tested and strengthened . . . . The Friends business meeting is not just the peculiar Quaker form of getting things done . . . it [is] an essential part of the spiritual formation . . . of every seasoned Friend, for it is that place through which we learn to walk hand in hand with each other and the Spirit out into the world to do the work of committed and obedient disciples.[52]

# 13

## COVENANT AND TESTIMONY

THE BASIC PREMISE of covenant in the Bible is that God has created an amazing world for us to live in—a garden to tend, as it is described in Genesis 2. And God abides with us as a teacher and mentor who is available, faithfully waiting for us to turn and be guided in how to live in this garden, how to tend it with the same wisdom with which it was created. That faithful abiding is God's covenant, a covenant of light and life, as early Friends sometimes called it. When we turn to the light and learn how to wait for its teaching day by day, we enter into covenantal faithfulness. We find ourselves growing into an open-ended relationship with God, with one another, and with the natural world.

All of our testimonies generate from that covenantal relationship. Indeed, like "calling" and "faithfulness," "testimony" or "witness" is a covenantal term. As mentioned in Chapter 11, the Hebrew word *adoth*, which is usually translated "testimony" or "witness," is sometimes translated "covenant." For example, in Exodus 31:18, the two stone tablets are referred to as the *adoth*, God's testimony, or covenant with Israel, mediated by Moses. Later, after the children of Israel have entered the Promised Land, Joshua renews the covenant with them, saying, the way you live in this land will be a testimony, *adoth*. Your lives will testify either for you or against you. Your actions will define your relationship with the Lord, "who has done you good" (Josh. 24:19-28). Indeed, the land itself is a witness to this covenant. Leviticus warns that if Israel lives out of harmony with one another and with the land, "the land will vomit you out" (Lev. 18:28).

This biblical tradition informs our Quaker understanding of testimony. Our actions communicate. The way we live reveals what we really believe, whatever we may say. Our actions either testify to the goodness we have learned from our inward teacher, or they testify against us. They reveal us to be hypocritical, superficial, not living from our center, from "that of God" in us.

"That of God in every one" is one of the most popular Quaker sound bites today. It's a term that George Fox seems to have coined and used many times. Rufus Jones re-introduced the term to Quaker usage a century ago. Today, we often affirm that "there is that of God in every one." True enough. But some years ago, the late T. Canby Jones pointed out that Fox rarely writes of "that of God in every one" just to affirm that it's there. He uses the term mainly in his epistles to Friends, where he repeatedly urges them to *answer* that of God in every one," to "reach to the witness in all." And he emphasizes that we do that at least as much by what we do, the way we live, how we carry ourselves, as what we say. This is the sense of one of his famous sayings, "let your lives preach." Consider this epistle written in 1656 to Friends in ministry as they began to fan out from Britain to the New World and to Europe and even the Middle East. It may be familiar to you. Fox writes,

[B]e patterns, be examples in all countries, places, islands, nations, wherever you come; that your carriage and life may preach among all sorts of people, and to them. Then you will come to walk cheerfully over the world, answering that of God in every one; whereby in them ye may be a blessing, and make the witness of God in them to bless you.[53]

In 17<sup>th</sup>-century usage, to "walk cheerfully" probably meant "walk courageous-ly." Friends needed courage as they ventured into many different cultures with their message in words and life. Fox also echoes here the covenant promise to Abraham, that by his descendants all the families of the earth would be blessed (see Gen. 12:1-4; 22:15-18).

So what comes from that of God in *us* communicates, it testifies, to that of God in *others*. It awakens the witness of God within and can turn people to begin living according to that witness. All of us have some experience of this in our own lives, how the words or actions of another person have caught our attention, awakened something in us that turned our lives in a powerful way.

But the opposite is just as true, as John Woolman warns in his 1763 essay, *A Plea for the Poor*:

> To conform a little to a wrong way strengthens the hands of such who carry wrong customs to their utmost extent; and the more a person appears to be virtuous and heavenly-minded, the more powerfully does his conformity operate in favour of evil-doers.[54]

Woolman adds that Friends are fond of claiming the moral high-ground. That makes our lapses all the more damaging.

In more modern times, John Punshon has written eloquently that testi-mony has both inward and outward dimensions:

> Inwardly, [the testimonies] are our guide to the nature of our Creator, the source of our inspiration, the medium of our understanding, the particular mystical path of Quakerism, our way to God. Externally, they are our guide to life, a sign of divine love for creation, the means of our prophetic witness. They therefore take their meaning from the highest reality we know.[55]

Our struggle is to make our testimony in life coherent and consistent—a life that communicates. John Conran, a 19th-century Irish Quaker minister, records in his journal his early struggle to give up fashionable clothing for plain Quaker dress. He writes that finally,

> I felt a solemn covering come over my spirit early one morning . . . to conform to the simple appearance of Christ's followers; His garment was all of a piece [John 19:23], so ought mine to be, of a piece with my speech, my life and conversation.[56]

Our Quaker dress has changed from plain to casual over the years. But many of us know the struggle for consistency that Conran describes, which may involve questions of where we buy our clothing, the labor relations involved in the making it, and so on. We struggle to make our lives "all of a piece," a living testimony that speaks *coherently* the divine goodness we have known in our lives and desire for others.

In a more contemporary statement (1994), British Friend Audrey Urry also speaks to the unity of testimony. She writes,

> All species and the Earth itself have interdependent roles within Creation. Humankind is not *the* species, to whom all others are subservient, but one among many. All parts, all issues, are inextricably intertwined. Indeed the web of creation could be described as of three-ply thread: wherever we touch it we affect justice and peace and the health of all everywhere. So all our testimonies, all our Quaker work, all our Quaker lives are part of one process, of striving toward a flourishing, just and peaceful Creation.[57]

All our testimonies are one testimony. SPICES makes a handy acronym for simplicity, peace, integrity, community, equality, and sustainability (or stewardship). But ultimately, our Quaker testimonies are not a mere checklist of things: they are different aspects of one reality—the one covenantal life we aspire to live.

This "unified field" of covenantal life is crucial today. We seek to live and communicate coherence amid a capitalist society that's organized by contracts, by narrowly defined, *quid pro quo*, self-interested agreements, where there is no forgiveness but only torts and settlements. These contractual arrangements become a *centrifugal* force tearing the creation apart economically, politically, socially—tearing us apart. Covenant is a *centripetal* force, drawing us together in reconciliation across our different identities and interests. It is the life of new beginnings. It is a gravitational force, drawing us back into a balanced relationship with the earth.

Testimony is our covenant-making activity in the world. It has three aspects. First, it's *ethical*: it's our discernment of the right thing to do, the right way to live—discerned by our sustained attention to the inward teacher, to our conversations with one another, to our Quaker processes of group decision-making, and to the hurt and hunger we encounter in the world. Second, it's *evangelical*. As Fox's epistle suggests, the integrity of our conduct and the prophetic truth of our witness draws others closer to the witness within themselves, their own inward teacher. Maybe they'll become Quakers. We should make that invitation sometimes. But the real concern is that others will draw closer in their way to what Fox called "the hidden unity of the Eternal Being."[58] Third and finally, as John Punshon's reflection intimates, our testimony is *sacramental*: our aim is to make everything we do an outward sign of the inward grace we have received. Some of the sacrament is ritual. Such rituals include the way we behave in the marketplace, recycle, compost and so on, day after day, week after week. But we also discern the sacrament in found moments between us, and sometimes in graced interactions with other species.

British Friend Jonathan Dale writes about a lifestyle-sharing group he initiated in his home meeting near Manchester. He quotes the reflection of one of the group's participants:

On a personal level, the lifestyle group was a way of getting closer to people at meeting, and hearing about their personal journeys. It made me more aware of the choices that I make every day and what assumptions lie behind my actions (not all of which are very Quakerly). I have made some changes in my life but I haven't, for example, got rid of my mobile phone. I haven't turned into an ascetic, nor do I think that this would be right for me. I've begun to realize, if only in a small way, the truth that the whole of our life is sacramental. Perhaps especially the boring, everyday bits (what we do with our rubbish, how we get to work, what we eat for our lunch). [59]

As we struggle toward a sustainable future, it's appropriate to think of sustainability as our faithful relationship with the earth and its species, faithful relationship of equity and peacefulness with others across society. All of these relationships grow and interweave a step at a time through faithful abiding with our inward teacher.

In the Gospel of John, Jesus makes the statement, "the one who sent me is true, and you do not know him" (John 7:28). He's not saying, "it's true, there is a God." That's a propositional truth. He means that God is true, God is faithful, ready to forgive, start over with us and lead us into a more authentic life. That's a truth we participate in as we answer God's faithfulness with our own. In the fifth chapter of John, Jesus heals a man paralyzed for 38 years, and he does it on the Sabbath. As he defends his action to his critics, Jesus makes some rather outrageous claims for himself and his relationship to God, creating a much larger scandal out of the incident. He answers his critics, saying he's not just bearing testimony to himself. He has witnesses to confirm his testimony. He cites his *actions*, which verify his words. He cites the *testimony of Moses*: the substance of the Torah confirms his words and actions. And finally, the *living word* within his accusers will confirm his testimony—if they will turn to it. Using one incident in the life of Jesus, John lays out how we know the truth. It's not just in the accuracy of what we say. It's confirmed by what we do, by the substance of the Scriptures, and by the quiet testimony of our inward teacher.[60]

The genius of Quaker faith and practice is that it continually consolidates and updates our testimony. It is a living testimony among us. It puts our words and our actions, our beliefs and our commitments, into a conversation that keeps winnowing truth out of delusion, faithfulness out of arbitrariness. It discerns the divine call out of the twittering Babel all around us.

# 14

---

## CAN'T SEE THE COVENANT FOR THE CONTRACTS

THE OLD SAYING "can't see the forest for the trees" expresses a key perceptual problem of human existence. We lose the *sense* of matters, even of life itself, as we get lost in the details. That perceptual pitfall can become a deadly spiritual malaise. We easily lose the Spirit of faith through our absorption in the letter of articulated belief. This is the all-too-familiar failing of all the great religions of the Book. But Eastern and New Age alternatives are not immune either. One may succumb to an enlightenment-by-the-numbers mentality just as easily as one falls prey to doctrinal dogmatism. Finally, there is a socioeconomic version of this age-old dilemma in our capitalist system. We routinely reduce God's creatures to marketable commodities. If we only see the trees— and if we see them only in board-feet—then we not only lose our sense of the forest; we soon lose the forest itself.

These dynamics apply to all forms of relationship. They make it difficult for us to recognize covenantal life within and around us. Covenant is faithful, loving relationship. It is the hidden, binding force of the universe. The Hebrew prophets were first to articulate what covenant is. They understood that covenant is the meaning and purpose behind all God's Creation. The universe exists to embody covenant. And covenant fulfills the purpose of each creature. To live in covenant is to be called, taught, led, and redeemed from senselessness by the same divine power that formed the galaxies. All life is part of this great covenantal drama, in which we struggle to act out faithful, loving roles with one another. In that sense, the universe is "the theater of God's glory," as John Calvin put it.

Like a forest, covenant is a complex ecology, an infinitely subtle network of relationships we struggle to maintain faithfully—with God, with ourselves, with one another, with the land on which we live. These relationships comprise a set of dialogues we carry on, in which we become accountable to one another, answerable for our words and actions. These relationships embody certain values, or virtues, not all of which we understand or can define. Some are in harmony with social norms, often making it easy to conform. Other values, especially those that have no market value, may be difficult to maintain in our culture. We may have to make sacrifices of worldly gain, status, or comfort to embody these values. But that is a part of being in covenant.

Particular realms of covenant are inevitably expressed in terms of principles, laws, or agreements. In science, they may be axiomatic laws of nature; in societies, they may be constitutions or compacts; in religious faiths, they may be doctrines and moral systems; in relationships, they may be marriage vows or other agreements. Martin Buber wrote that covenant is first, last, and always the "lived relationship" between its parties. But the explicit understandings and agreements that evolve through the relationship are important.

For example, the faithful love between parent and child is always accompanied by serious boundaries to be respected and expectations to be fulfilled. Parents limit the children and children limit the parents. These limits often become sources of conflict and negotiation in family life. Family members may struggle at times to see the covenantal love undergirding the many agreements. Yet it is there, infusing it all, hoping beyond expectation, forgiving lapses.

A local faith community—a Friends meeting, for example—is rife with understandings, rituals, and norms: the handshake at the close of meeting, or who is responsible to lock the building after meeting. Understandings like these, both tacit and explicit, make up the warp and weft of a meeting's fabric. Sometimes our struggle with one another over these particulars pushes our patience to the limit. Yet at some level, we know that the real life of the meeting exists both within and beyond all these arrangements. It is that secret life in covenantal trust, lived out through the promises we make and keep, that hopefully carries us together through it all.

A good business does not only demonstrate integrity in all its contracts. It also embodies a larger fidelity to people, values, and the physical environment beyond the interested parties of any given contract. Any business must struggle to maintain that fidelity in the face of competition from other businesses that do not uphold these larger values. It is tempting to put on the moral "blinders" of the limited contract, a *quid pro quo* agreement between interested parties, without any necessary concern for others and a hidden proviso that "the devil take the hindmost." But businesses of integrity find another way.

Perhaps it is not surprising that God's great covenant partner, Israel, bears a name meaning "wrestler with God." Because it is dialogical, covenant always includes struggle. Yet the fruit of covenant struggle, according to Hebrew Scripture, is *shalom*, a "peace" that is more vibrant, integrative, and all-encompassing than the usual connotations of our English word (see the definitions of *shalom* in Chapter 11). It is the peace that surpasses all our understandings.

Early Friends wrote of the "covenant of light, life, and peace" they had found together. The light was their lived relationship with God and with one another. It brought them to a peace they had never before known. The early Quaker understanding of the light was strongly covenantal. They witnessed the covenant of light shining forth in all people, everywhere, undergirding everything.

Yet that very quality of omnipresence means that the light is also hidden to us. We are like fish living in the sea, not knowing what water is. So it is often by some experience of desertion, darkness, or faithlessness that we begin to know the covenant of light explicitly. The loss of a loved one, the failure of a marriage, unemployment, or an experience of betrayal drives us into a place of darkness. Hopefully, our eyes will eventually begin to perceive a subtle light there. It is always there, but we are unable to see it until our constructed world of understandings and agreements falls apart. That light is the covenant. It abides within and beyond each of us, within and beyond every faithful relationship, within and beyond every good human hope. By that light, we may begin to rebuild our lives.

▲ ▲ ▲

The capitalist social and economic system that now dominates our entire planet is a remarkably creative regime. Its contractual method of organization has progressively been applied to all realms of society—from market economics to democratic politics to religious pluralism. It has created an elastic, polymorphous structure, allowing the peoples of the world to interact in unprecedented ways. Over its four centuries of development, capitalism has exerted a permanent state of revolution on every society where it takes hold. And the speed of economic expansion and integration only seems to accelerate.

But like most revolutions and their ruling regimes, capitalism has its destructive side. And as the revolution accelerates, so does the destruction. The massive scale of human exploitation that keeps capitalism expanding has produced mind-numbing suffering and social blight. In particular, poor nations and the poor sectors of our society bear the "hidden" costs of affluence in the United States and other wealthy nations. Moreover, the simple arithmetic of continued capitalist expansion on a planet of limited resources and fragile ecological balances inexorably adds up to the physical and spiritual degradation of our planet and all of us on it. Even those of us living in this vast system's more privileged sectors feel its ravages on the life we hold sacred. The upwardly mobile often pay dearly for their ascent in terms of their spiritual, family, and community lives. We see it everywhere.

Capitalism poses as a relatively value-free system, creating opportunity in all directions for all participants. But because the system is weighted in favor of those who possess capital resources, it tends to carry inherited, pernicious biases along with it. Thus, although capitalism is not inherently racist or sexist, it has accommodated and magnified those inequities for centuries. Only as the market has needed the wider participation of minorities and women—both as producers and as consumers—has capitalist society decided that they deserve a better chance to play the game.

Technology is the darling child of capitalism, which has fostered its development as no other economic system has in history. Technology too poses as morally neutral. After all, a tool is subject to whatever designs are upon the mind of the one who wields it, right? But as society becomes increasingly elaborate technologically, it becomes a force with a life of its own. Like capitalism, technology is a *means* that tends to reshape the *ends* to which it is exerted. Noble ends—socially conscious and environmentally responsible—are easily subverted by the tempting possibility of achieving other ends more quickly, easily, or profitably. When Apple's iPad was first introduced, a man in line waiting to buy one was asked what he planned to do with it. He responded that he wasn't sure, but he would find out when he got it. The quip "iPad, therefore I am" insinuates the way our highly mediated, interconnected world is transforming our consciousness.

Yet we continue to be naively surprised that the system has somehow cast off or left behind people, values, lands, and species that we hold dear. We feel compelled to defend them, yet find ourselves always on the defensive, reacting to the latest horror story of injustice, violence, or pollution.

There are many struggles to be waged socially and politically against the blights of the system that engulfs us so totally. But if we wish to move beyond a reactive political posture, *let us reclaim a sense of covenant.* Covenant is not a super-theory defining everything. It is not a master plan for a new society. Rather, it is a sense of the whole, a sense of integrity that keeps sight of the forest, and of one's place in it. Covenant is a web of faithful, accountable relationships as complex and polymorphous as capitalism itself—even more so. It does not simply shrug off the people, values, and species that find no value in the market, but insists that there be room for everyone. Covenant is the only thing left that is still larger than the global Babel we have helped build.

Covenant is a crucial understanding for us to reclaim today, precisely because it is intimately related to the contractual culture of capitalism. In fact, covenant was a key intellectual factor in the development of capitalism. During the Reformation era, the Protestant concern to restructure the Church as a covenantal community spun off reevaluations of all realms of society. In economic life, covenant helped inform the contractual basis of a market society. In science, the covenantal sense of God's well-ordered Creation influenced the early search for dependable laws governing nature. In political thought, covenant helped nurture the social contract theories that gave rise to the modern democratic state. Thus, on many fronts, covenant is the forgotten utopian motive behind the edifice of modernity. It needs to be reclaimed, if we are to correct the course that society has taken.

In *The Covenant Crucified: Quakers and the Rise of Capitalism* (Pendle Hill, 1995), I explored the role of early Friends in the beginnings of our modern, capitalist era. Through their prophetic preaching and their alternative social ordering, Quakers charted a covenantal course for capitalist society. They had a covenantal sense of direction for the new regime. The heroic sacrifices made by these ordinary men and women to win the hearts and minds of their neighbors and rulers underscores the holy, covenantal nature of their calling. It is a powerful saga, bittersweet in the sense of the hope that lived and died in those first years of Quaker witness. Yet it offers us a glimpse, not only of a fuller Quaker vision, but of a larger, covenantal social vision to be rediscovered and reenacted today.

No book can reveal the reality of covenant. Neither can this essay. Only the grace of God can do that. But part of that revealing process is to unmask

the regime that we assume to be self-evident and without alternatives. To rediscover the forest is to look both at and beyond the trees. Rediscovering covenant begins with seeing through the contractual culture that surrounds us.

# CODA

## HOSPITALITY:
## THE PRACTICE OF COVENANTAL FAITHFULNESS

ONE OF MY most well-used books is Henri Nouwen's *Bread for the Journey: A Daybook of Wisdom and Faith*, written near the end of his life.[61] I've read it through four or five times now. Each day offers a short reminder of the basics of a Christian faith, which Nouwen nuanced with valuable psychological insights. In the early March readings, he connects *covenant* with *hospitality* and *calling*, which had new significance for me as I completed this book.

As I continue to reflect on those connections, several things occur that amplify the themes of this book. In his early classic, *Reaching Out*, Nouwen defines hospitality as "the creation of a free space where the stranger can enter and become a friend instead of an enemy. Hospitality is not to change people, but to offer them space where change can take place."[62] Thinking of hospitality as covenant-practice, we can see it begin as we create free space within ourselves for the *inward teacher*, a stranger who has long awaited our attention. We maintain that space as we learn how to devote time and attention to discerning the subtle counsel of the light. As we dare to follow the light's leadings, we open new spaces, places we were fearful to enter, or perhaps never even noticed before. We find ourselves led into deeper levels of *conversation* with others, where we invite their truth. Nouwen writes,

To listen is very hard, because it asks of us so much interior stability that we no longer need to prove ourselves by speeches, arguments, statements, or declarations. . . . Listening is paying full attention to others and welcoming them into our very beings. . . . Listening is a form of spiritual hospitality by which you invite strangers to become friends, to get to know their inner selves more fully, and even to dare to be silent with you.[63]

Those who have learned hospitality to the inward teacher and in listening to others will readily find a home in the quiet of Quaker *meeting for worship*. They will understand their part in creating and holding the sacred space of worship among us. Otherwise, without the covenantal life-practice of listening, one hour of meeting for worship on Sundays amounts to little more than a thin wafer of communion that one can happily miss most weeks, or forsake altogether.

Holding the space of covenantal relationship is often raised to its highest practice in the *meeting for worship for business*. Here listening deeply to one another is crucial to any hope of reaching Spirit-led decisions. Listening for "where the words come from," is as important as hearing the words themselves. That deeper discernment opens a space among us that frees us from judging the words, to hear more generously the spirit behind them. It's our spiritual hospitality toward one another. Not all contributions will lead toward the unity that ultimately emerges in the group. But the space for those hopes, concerns, and side-bars will have been maintained—and they may prove more important in hindsight than they seemed at the time. Hence, spiritual hospitality is a space-time continuum, just as covenant is a living faith carried on from generation to generation. The prophet ignored in one generation may become an important voice a generation or more later, as we listen to our ancestors in the faith.

Our Quaker *testimonies* are words, actions, and lifestyle choices that "answer that of God in every one." When we connect in that way with others, whether friends or strangers, a covenantal space of learning and potential change opens up within and between us. We may feel invited, challenged, or confronted in those moments. But when the spirit of hospitality is maintained, there is room for both sides to move and change. Later in *Reaching Out*, Nouwen adds an important corollary to his definition of hospitality:

> Receptivity is only one side of hospitality. The other side, equally important, is confrontation. . . . Real receptivity asks for confrontation because space can only be a welcoming space when there are clear boundaries, and boundaries are limits between which we define our own position. Flexible limits, but limits nonetheless. Confrontation results from the articulate presence, the presence within boundaries."[64]

Our Quaker testimonies articulate our boundaries, often through the activities we renounce, the social conformities we resist, the honors or privileges we refuse. But the intention within those boundaries is *friendship*, nonviolent communication, and the hope of reconciliation. Friendship is part of the genius of Quaker faith and practice, because it invites others, across all kinds of social and religious differences, into the space of our common humanity. Friendship extends even beyond our species to others. That kind of social and species transcendence is grounded and strengthened in the practice of befriending the inward, divine teacher.

Clearly, this is not a general code of ethics. Our covenantal faithfulness plays out as we discern and answer our unique, divine *calling* in the world. Nouwen notes how paralyzing and depressing the problems of the world can become to us:

> Here the word *call* becomes important. We are not called to save the world, solve all problems, and help all people. But each of us has our own unique call, in our families, in our work, in our world. We have to keep asking God to help us see clearly what our call is and to give us the strength to live out that call with trust. Then we will discover

that our faithfulness to a small task is the most healing response to the illnesses of our time.[65]

As we live into our calls, we learn the truth of Jesus' call down through the ages: "Come to me, you who labor and are heavy-laden. . . . My yoke is easy, my burden is light" (Matt. 11:28-30). The call clears a space within the blizzard of concerns that swirls around us, and shows us next steps on a path of faithfulness.

It is important to remember that our testimonies are primarily the ways we speak, act, and live in the world, rather than a set of social values and political positions. But as we live into the testimonies, we find ourselves called to assert them in larger social spaces. We become advocates for the full social inclusion and political rights of people of all faiths, races, genders, and classes. The constitutional space of civil society is not the same as the covenantal space of faith communities, but our communities have a crucial role in making the constitutional space more fully civil and equal, because we bring a transcendent perspective. In the light, we can see people as not only equal but beloved.

We also find ourselves drawn to protect rivers, seas, lakes, forests, mountains, and meadows as sacred trusts, covenantal spaces. As humans have become so dominant on the earth, the natural world is no longer a wilderness to be tamed but a community of species needing our hospitality, and habitats to be preserved as sacred spaces. Again, faith communities often see this most clearly because of our transcendent perspective. We see the natural world as a divine creation, the realm where God's purposes are revealed and realized. To repeat the opening of the last chapter, we see the forest, not only the trees; the trees and not only the board-feet that sawing could produce to sell in the marketplace.

*Sanctuary* is another name for the varieties of covenantal space we contemplate here. Science analyzes the natural and social worlds into smaller and smaller bits; technology rationalizes every purpose into a step-by-step process; the market capitalizes all matter and culture into commodified forms; political and legal processes attempt to adjudicate between proliferating identities and interests. Amid all of this, there is a growing cry in the world for sanctuary, a haven of wholeness. It is true that covenant can become reactionary if it simply draws back from every advance of science, technology, economy, and politics. But it becomes radical, at times even revolutionary, when it creatively reasserts wholeness and sacred space in light of new developments.

That movement can take the form of outright resistance. For example, the sanctuary movement of the 1980s, which aided and sheltered political refugees from Central America, amounted to *civil disobedience* in regard to federal law. But the Quaker sanctuary leader Jim Corbett preferred the term *civil initiative*, because these churches and synagogues were asserting international laws guaranteeing the protection of political refugees. Corbett made use of the term covenant, partly from his training as a political theorist, and partly from his dialogue with Christians and Jews in the sanctuary movement.

In more recent years, the Occupy movement (noted briefly in Chapter 6) arose as a spontaneous convergence of many different groups and individuals motivated by a variety of concerns, to assert a covenantal presence around financial centers such as Wall Street, and to "call out" the financial interests that had toyed so carelessly with the economic well-being of America and the world. As this book comes to completion, the convergence of many different groups with the Sioux people at Standing Rock, South Dakota confronts the increasingly risky methods of maintaining our dependence upon fossil fuels. In protecting the waters there against likely contamination by pipeline oil, sanctuary is being asserted against the headlong rush of natural resource extraction and the finance capital that drives it.

It is my prayer that readers will sit with the wide-ranging reflections gathered into this book, discern the wholeness that has drawn them together, and find some encouragement in following their own calls to radical faithfulness.

# NOTES

1. Gwyn, *Words in Time: Essays and Addresses* (Bellefonte, PA: Kimo Press, 1997); also available online: quakertheology.org/GwynBook–RV-12-2015.pdf.

2. George Fox, *The Journal of George Fox*, John L. Nickalls, ed. (Cambridge: Cambridge University Press, 1952), p. 11.

3. Fox, *Journal,* pp. 69-70.

4. James Nayler, *Works,* vol. 1 (Glenside, PA: Quaker Heritage Press, 2003), pp. 33-34.

5. Margaret Fell, "The testimony of Margaret Fox concerning her late husband," in George Fox, *Journal* (1694), p. ii; reprinted in Britain Yearly Meeting, *Quaker Faith & Practice* (London: Quaker Books, 1995), 19.07.

6. Margaret Fell, *A collection of remarkable passages relating to . . . Margaret Fell* (1710); reprinted in Britain Yearly Meeting, *Quaker Faith & Practice,* 19:38.

7. Fell, *Women's Speaking Justified* (London, 1666), reprinted by New England Yearly Meeting, 1980, p. 12. The full text can also be found online at qhpress.org/texts/fell. Fox published a shorter tract, *The Woman Learning in Silence,* in 1656, containing some of the same points, but Fell's is the fullest early Quaker treatment of the subject.

8. For these and other details of Ann Audland's story, see W. C. Braithwaite, *The Beginnings of Quakerism* London: Macmillan, 1912), pp. 199-200; and Ernest Taylor, *The Valiant Sixty* (London: Bannisdale, 1951), pp. 27-28.

9. The incident is described by Stephen Crisp in his "Testimony concerning James Parnell," Parnell, *Works,* (1675).

10. Quoted in Braithwaite, *Beginnings*, p. 191.

11. David J. Garrow, *Bearing the Cross: Martin Luther King, Jr. and the Southern Christian Leadership Conference*, 1987.

12. John Burnyeat, "An Account of John Burnyeat's Convincement," in his collected works, *Truth Exalted* (London, 1691); also in the *Friends Library*, vol. 11, p. 122 (*Friends Library* also available on Google Books).

13. Unless noted otherwise, all quotations from the Bible are from the New Revised Standard Version.

14. Arthur O. Waskow and Phyllis O. Berman, *Freedom Journeys: The Tale of Exodus and Wilderness across Millennia* (Woodstock, VT: Jewish Lights, 2011), Chapter 1.

15. For more, see the trailer for *Transfigurations: Transgressing Gender in the Bible* at petersontoscano.com.

16. For more on the Ranters, see Gwyn, *Seekers Found: Atonement in Early Quaker Experience* (Wallingford, PA: Pendle Hill, 2000), Chapter 6.

17. Sarah Jones, *This is Lights appearance in the Truth* (London, 1650); reprinted in *Hidden in Plain Sight*, Mary Garman, et. al., eds. (Wallingford, PA: Pendle Hill, 1995), pp. 35-37. For more on Sarah Jones, see Gwyn, *Seekers Found*, Chapter 7.

18. Sarah Blackborow, *A Visit to the Spirit in Prison* (London, 1658); reprinted in *Hidden in Plain Sight*, pp. 47-57.

19. Francis Howgill, *The Inheritance of Jacob Discovered* (London, 1655), p. 45.

20. Richard Gregg, *The Power of Nonviolence*, quoted in Gwyn, *Personality and Place: The Life and Times of Pendle Hill* (Philadelphia: Plain Press, 2014), pp. 68-69.

21. These two kinds of Seekers are profiled in Chapter 4 of *Seekers Found*, previously cited.

22. See also Fox, *Journal*, p. 87.

23. Fox, *Journal*, p. 121.

24. Gwyn, *Apocalypse of the Word: The Life and Message of George Fox* (Richmond, IN: Friends United Press, 1986, 2015).

25. Norman K. Gottwald, *The Tribes of Yahweh: A Sociology of the Religion of Liberated Israel, 1250-1050 B. C. E.* (Maryknoll, NY: Orbis, 1979), Chapter 45.

26. See Adela Yarbro Collins, *Crisis and Catharsis: The Power of the Apocalypse* (Philadelphia: Westminster, 1984), Chapter 1.

27. William Penn, *The Rise and Progress of the People Called Quakers* (London, 1694), reprinted in *The Witness of William* Penn, Frederick B. Tolles and Gordon Alderfer, eds. (New York: Macmillan, 1957), p. 29.

28. For a fuller treatment of the Nayler crisis as the defining moment of the Lamb's War, see Gwyn, *The Covenant Crucified*, Chapter 5.

29. James Nayler, *Works*, vol. 4 (Glenside, PA: Quaker Heritage Press, 2009), pp. 3-9.

30. Gwyn, *The Anti-War: Peace Finds the Purpose of a Peculiar People/Militant Peacemaking in the Manner of Friends* (San Francisco: Inner Light Books, 2016).

31. Mary Morrison, *Approaching the Gospels,* Pendle Hill Pamphlet #219 (Wallingford, PA: Pendle Hill, 1978).

32. Fox, *Journal*, p. 11.

33. John Woolman, *Journal and Major Essays,* Phillips Moulton, ed. (New York: Oxford University Press, 1971), p. 133.

34. Fox, *Journal*, p. xliv.

35. Fox, *Journal*, p. 437.

36. Fox, *Journal*, p. 759.

37. Gwyn, *The Covenant Crucified: Quakers and the Rise or Capitalism* (Wallingford, PA: Pendle Hill, 1995; reprinted London: Quaker Books, 2006).

38. Gerhard von Rad, *Old Testament Theology* (New York: Harper, 1962), vol. 1, p. 130.

39. Isaac Penington, *A Brief Account of my Soul's Travel Towards the Holy Land* (1668), in Penington, *Works*, vol. 3 (Glenside, PA: Quaker Heritage Press), pp. 99-105. For more on Isaac and Mary Penington, see Gwyn, *Seekers Found*, Chapter 9.

40. Sarah Jones, *This Is Lights Appearance* (1650), cited earlier.

41. Howgill, *The Inheritance of Jacob Discovered.*

42. Thomas Kelly, *A Testament of Devotion* (New York: Harper & Row, 1941), pp. 29-32.

43. Rex Ambler, *Light to Live By* (London: Quaker Books, 2001), p. 47.

44. See Braithwaite, *The Beginnings of Quakerism*, p. 199. Also see Richard Bauman, *Let Your Words Be Few: Symbolism of Speaking and Silence among Seventeenth-Century Quakers* (Cambridge: Cambridge University Press, 1983), p. 40.

45. Mary Penington, *The Experiences in the Life of Mary Penington* (1821), reprinted by Friends Historical Society (London, 1992), p. 45.

46. Howgill, "Testimony Concerning Edward Burrough," in Burrough's *Works* (London, 1672); reprinted in Britain Yearly Meeting, *Quaker Faith & Practice*, 19.08.

47. Thomas Kelly, "The Gathered Meeting," in *The Eternal Promise* (Richmond, IN: Friends United Press, 1966), pp. 72, 87.

48. Martin Buber, as quoted in Janet E. Schroeder, *Dialogue with the Other: Martin Buber and the Quaker Experience,* Pendle Hill Pamphlet #192 (Wallingford, PA: Pendle Hill, 1973), p. 18.

49. Kelly, "The Gathered Meeting," p. 89.

50. William Taber, *Four Doors to Meeting for Worship*, Pendle Hill Pamphlet #306 (Wallingford, PA, 1992), pp. 25-26.

51. Edward Burrough, "A Testimony concerning the beginning of the work of the Lord" (1662), quoted in Britain Yearly Meeting, *Quaker Faith & Practice*, 1995, 2.87.

52. William Taber, *The Mind of Christ,* Pendle Hill Pamphlet #406 (Wallingford, PA: Pendle Hill, 2010), pp. 6-7.

53. Fox, *Journal*, p. 263.

54. John Woolman, *A Plea for the* Poor (1763), in Woolman, *Journal and Major Essays*, , pp. 247-48.

55. John Punshon, *Testimony and Tradition*, 1990 Swarthmore Lecture (London: Quaker Home Service, 1990), p. 94.

56. John Conran, *Journal* (1877), p. 26.

57. Audrey Urry, quoted in Britain Yearly Meeting, *Quaker Faith & Practice*, 1995, 25.04.

58. Fox, *Journal*, p. 28.

59. Jonathan Dale, *Quaker Social Testimony in Personal and Corporate Life*, Pendle Hill Pamphlet #360 (Wallingford, PA: Pendle Hill, 2002), p. 20.

60. For a fuller treatment of this story, see Gwyn, *Conversation with Christ: Quaker Meditations on the Gospel of John* (Philadelphia: Quaker Press, 2011), Chapter 4.

61. Henri J. M. Nouwen, *Bread for the Journey: A Daybook of Wisdom and Faith* (San Francisco: HarperCollins, 1997).

62. Nouwen, *Reaching Out: The Three Movements of the Spiritual Life* (New York: Doubleday, 1975), p. 71.

63. Nouwen, *Bread*, March 11.

64. Nouwen, *Reaching Out*, p. 98.

65. Nouwen, *Bread*, March 10.